TIMED READINGS

Third Edition

Fifty 400-Word Passages
with Questions for
Building Reading Speed

BOOK TEN

Edward Spargo

JAMESTOWN PUBLISHERS

a division of NTC/CONTEMPORARY PUBLISHING GROUP
Lincolnwood, Illinois USA

Titles in This Series
Timed Readings, Third Edition
Timed Readings in Literature

Teaching Notes are available for this text and
will be sent to the instructor. Please write on
school stationery; tell us what grade
you teach and identify the text.

Timed Readings, Third Edition
Book Ten

Cover and text design: Deborah Hulsey Christie

ISBN: 0-89061-512-8

Published by Jamestown Publishers,
a division of NTC/Contemporary Publishing Group, Inc.,
4255 West Touhy Avenue,
Lincolnwood (Chicago), Illinois 60712-1975 U.S.A.
© 1989 by NTC/Contemporary Publishing Group, Inc.
10 11 12 13 14 15 16 17 18 19 20 021 09 08 07 06 05 04 03 02 01

Contents

Introduction to the Student

These *Timed Readings* are designed to help you become a faster and better reader. As you progress through the book, you will find yourself growing in reading speed and comprehension. You will be challenged to increase your reading rate while maintaining a high level of comprehension.

Reading, like most things, improves with practice. If you practice improving your reading speed, you will improve. As you will see, the rewards of improved reading speed will be well worth your time and effort.

Why Read Faster?

The quick and simple answer is that faster readers are better readers. Does this statement surprise you? You might think that fast readers would miss something and their comprehension might suffer. This is not true, for two reasons:

1. Faster readers comprehend faster. When you read faster, the writer's message is coming to you faster and makes sense sooner. Ideas are interconnected. The writer's thoughts are all tied together, each one leading to the next. The more quickly you can see how ideas are related to each other, the more quickly you can comprehend the meaning of what you are reading.

2. Faster readers concentrate better. Concentration is essential for comprehension. If your mind is wandering you can't understand what you are reading. A lack of concentration causes you to re-read, sometimes over and over, in order to comprehend. Faster readers concentrate better because there's less time for distractions to interfere. Comprehension, in turn, contributes to concentration. If you are concentrating and comprehending, you will not become distracted.

Want to Read More?

Do you wish that you could read more? (or, at least, would you like to do your required reading in less time?) Faster reading will help.

The illustration on the next page shows the number of books someone might read over a period of ten years. Let's see what faster reading could do for you. Look at the stack of books read by a slow reader and the stack

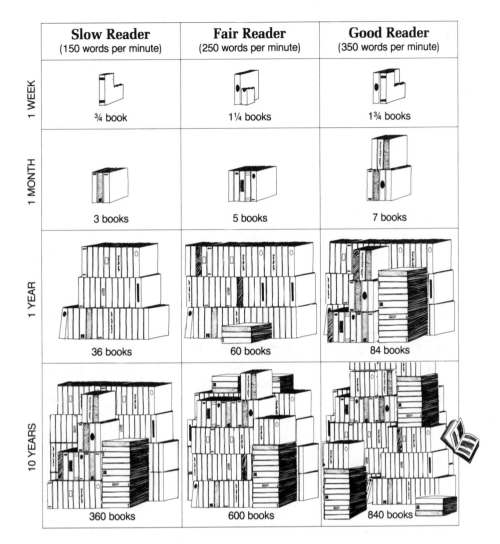

	Slow Reader (150 words per minute)	Fair Reader (250 words per minute)	Good Reader (350 words per minute)
1 WEEK	¾ book	1¼ books	1¾ books
1 MONTH	3 books	5 books	7 books
1 YEAR	36 books	60 books	84 books
10 YEARS	360 books	600 books	840 books

read by a good reader. (We show a speed of 350 words a minute for our "good" reader, but many fast readers can more than double that speed.) Let's say, however, that you are now reading at a rate of 150 words a minute. The illustration shows you reading 36 books a year. By increasing your reading speed to 250 words a minute, you could increase the number of books to 60 a year.

We have arrived at these numbers by assuming that the readers in our illustration read for one hour a day, six days a week, and that an average book is about 72,000 words long. Many people do not read that much, but they might if they could learn to read better and faster.

Faster reading doesn't *take* time, it *saves* time!

How to Use This Book

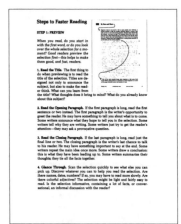

1 **Learn the Four Steps**
Study and learn the four steps to follow to become a better and faster reader. The steps are covered on pages 9, 10, 11, and 12.

2 **Preview**
Turn to the selection you are going to read and wait for the instructor's signal to preview. Your instructor will allow 30 seconds for previewing.

3 **Begin reading**
When your instructor gives you the signal, begin reading. Read at a slightly faster-than-normal speed. Read well enough so that you will be able to answer questions about what you have read.

7 **Fill in the progress gra**
Enter your score and plot your reading time on the graph on page 118 or 119. The right-hand side o the graph shows your words-per-minute reading speed. Write this number at the bottom of the page on the line labeled *Words per Minute*.

4 **Record your time**
When you finish reading, look at the black-board and note your reading time. Your reading time will be the lowest time remaining on the board, or the next number to be erased. Write this time at the bottom of the page on the line labeled *Reading Time.*

5 **Answer the questions**
Answer the ten questions on the next page. There are five fact questions and five thought questions. Pick the *best* answer to each question and put an x in the box beside it.

6 **Correct your answers**
Using the Answer Key on pages 116 and 117, correct your work. Circle your wrong answers and put an x in the box you should have marked. Score 10 points for each correct answer. Write your score at the bottom of the page on the line labeled *Comprehension Score.*

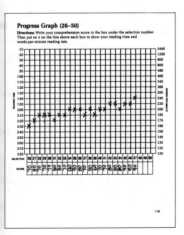

Progress Graph (26–50)

Directions: Write your comprehension score in the box under the selection number. Then put an x on the line above each box to show your reading time and words-per-minute reading rate.

Instructions for the Pacing Drills

From time to time your instructor may wish to conduct pacing drills using *Timed Readings*. For this work you need to use the Pacing Dots printed in the margins of your book pages. The dots will help you regulate your reading speed to match the pace set by your instructor or announced on the reading cassette tape.

Pacing Dots

You will be reading at the correct pace if you are at the dot when your instructor says "Mark" or when you hear a tone on the tape. If you are ahead of the pace, read a little more slowly; if you are behind the pace, increase your reading speed. Try to match the pace exactly.

Follow these steps.

Step 1: Record the pace. At the bottom of the page, write on the line labeled *Words per Minute* the rate announced by the instructor or by the speaker on the tape.

Step 2: Begin reading. Wait for the signal to begin reading. Read at a slightly faster-than-normal speed. You will not know how on-target your pace is until you hear your instructor say "Mark" or until you hear the first tone on the tape. After a little practice you will be able to select an appropriate starting speed most of the time.

Step 3: Adjust your pace. As you read, try to match the pace set by the instructor or the tape. Read more slowly or more quickly as necessary. You should be reading the line beside the dot when you hear the pacing signal. The pacing sounds may distract you at first. Don't worry about it. Keep reading and your concentration will return.

Step 4: Stop and answer questions. Stop reading when you are told to, even if you have not finished the selection. Answer the questions right away. Correct your work and record your score on the line *Comprehension Score*. Strive to maintain 80 percent comprehension on each drill as you gradually increase your pace.

Step 5: Fill in the pacing graph. Transfer your words-per-minute rate to the box labeled *Pace* on the pacing graph on page 120. Then plot your comprehension score on the line above the box.

These pacing drills are designed to help you become a more flexible reader. They encourage you to "break out" of a pattern of reading everything at the same speed.

The drills help in other ways, too. Sometimes in a reading program you reach a certain level and bog down. You don't seem able to move on and progress. The pacing drills will help you to work your way out of such slumps and get your reading program moving again.

Steps to Faster Reading

STEP 1: PREVIEW

When you read, do you start in with the first word, or do you look over the whole selection for a moment? Good readers preview the selection first—this helps to make them good, and fast, readers.

1. Read the Title. The first thing to do when previewing is to read the title of the selection. Titles are designed not only to announce the subject, but also to make the reader think. What can you learn from the title? What thoughts does it bring to mind? What do you already know about this subject?

2. Read the Opening Paragraph. If the first paragraph is long, read the first sentence or two instead. The first paragraph is the writer's opportunity to greet the reader. He may have something to tell you about what is to come. Some writers announce what they hope to tell you in the selection. Some writers tell why they are writing. Some writers just try to get the reader's attention—they may ask a provocative question.

3. Read the Closing Paragraph. If the last paragraph is long, read just the final line or two. The closing paragraph is the writer's last chance to talk to his reader. He may have something important to say at the end. Some writers repeat the main idea once more. Some writers draw a conclusion: this is what they have been leading up to. Some writers summarize their thoughts; they tie all the facts together.

4. Glance Through. Scan the selection quickly to see what else you can pick up. Discover whatever you can to help you read the selection. Are there names, dates, numbers? If so, you may have to read more slowly. Are there colorful adjectives? The selection might be light and fairly easy to read. Is the selection informative, containing a lot of facts, or conversational, an informal discussion with the reader?

---

22 By Sun and Stars

Migratory birds do not travel as fast as some people once believed. A German scientist in 1895, for example, attributed speeds in excess of 200 miles an hour to some birds during migration. Research later showed that this estimate was much too high. The peregrine falcon flies 165 to 180 miles per hour while chasing food, but very few birds can fly this fast. Birds have two speeds. One is for normal flying, and a faster one is for escaping enemies or chasing food. Most songbirds have cruising speeds between 25 and 50 miles per hour during migration.

One of the most amazing things about migration is that some birds raised without adult guidance or experience in actual migration can orient to the proper direction across vast stretches of water.

Reading Time_____ Comprehension Score_____ Words per Minute_____ 57

flying
normal
towers
stage
migration.
some
cruising
pelicans,
time
subtle
scientists
close

Steps to Faster Reading

STEP 2: READ FOR MEANING

When you read, do you just see words? Are you so occupied reading words that you sometimes fail to get the meaning? Good readers see beyond the words—they read for meaning. This makes them faster readers.

1. Build Concentration. You cannot read with understanding if you are not concentrating. Every reader's mind wanders occasionally; it is not a cause for alarm. When you discover that your thoughts have strayed, correct the situation right away. The longer you wait, the harder it becomes. Avoid distractions and distracting situations. Outside noises and activities will compete for your attention if you let them. Keep the preview information in mind as you read. This will help to focus your attention on the selection.

2. Read in Thought Groups. Individual words do not tell us much. They must be combined with other words in order to yield meaning. To obtain meaning from the printed page, therefore, the reader should see the words in meaningful combinations. If you see only a word at a time (called word-by-word reading), your comprehension suffers along with your speed. To improve both speed and comprehension, try to group the words into phrases which have a natural relationship to each other. For practice, you might want to read aloud, trying to speak the words in meaningful combinations.

3. Question the Author. To sustain the pace you have set for yourself, and to maintain a high level of comprehension, question the writer as you read. Continually ask yourself such questions as, "What does this mean? What is he saying now? How can I use this information?" Questions like these help you to concentrate fully on the selection.

Steps to Faster Reading

STEP 3: GRASP PARAGRAPH SENSE

The paragraph is the basic unit of meaning. If you can discover quickly and understand the main point of each paragraph, you can comprehend the author's message. Good readers know how to find the main ideas of paragraphs quickly. This helps to make them faster readers.

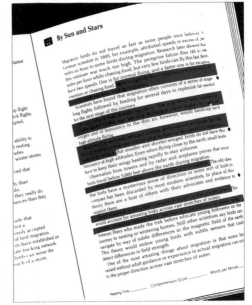

1. Find the Topic Sentence. The topic sentence, the sentence containing the main idea, is often the first sentence of a paragraph. It is followed by other sentences which support, develop, or explain the main idea. Sometimes a topic sentence comes at the end of a paragraph. When it does, the supporting details come first, building the base for the topic sentence. Some paragraphs do not have a topic sentence. Such paragraphs usually create a mood or feeling, rather than present information.

2. Understand Paragraph Structure. Every well-written paragraph has purpose. The purpose may be to inform, define, explain, persuade, compare or contrast, illustrate, and so on. The purpose should always relate to the main idea and expand on it. As you read each paragraph, see how the body of the paragraph is used to tell you more about the main idea or topic sentence. Read the supporting details intelligently, recognizing that what you are reading is all designed to develop the single main idea.

Steps to Faster Reading

STEP 4: ORGANIZE FACTS

When you read, do you tend to see a lot of facts without any apparent connection or relationship? Understanding how the facts all fit together to deliver the author's message is, after all, the reason for reading. Good readers organize facts as they read. This helps them to read rapidly and well.

1. Discover the Writer's Plan. Look for a clue or signal word early in the article which might reveal the author's structure. Every writer has a plan or outline which he follows. If the reader can discover his method of organization, he has the key to understanding the message. Sometimes the author gives you obvious signals. If he says, "There are three reasons . . ." the wise reader looks for a listing of the three items. Other less obvious signal words such as *moreover, otherwise, consequently* all tell the reader the direction the writer's message will take.

2. Relate as You Read. As you read the selection, keep the information learned during the preview in mind. See how the ideas you are reading all fit into place. Consciously strive to relate what you are reading to the title. See how the author is carrying through in his attempt to piece together a meaningful message. As you discover the relationship among the ideas, the message comes through quickly and clearly.

Timed
Reading
Selections

1   The Best of the Palaces

India has thousands of architectural masterpieces representing many styles and periods. The most famous of these is a marble monument in Agra which for centuries has drawn travelers across the desert to stand before it in awe.

The Taj Mahal has inspired works of literature and music, and seems to symbolize India to the world, yet few know what it actually is. This elegant, perfectly proportioned building, whose name roughly translates as "best of the palaces" is a mausoleum for the wife of the famous Moghul emperor Shah Jahan.

Arjuman Banu Begum, who after marriage was renamed Mumtaz Mahal, or "the exalted of the palace," was much beloved by the emperor and by her subjects. Her generosity, kindness, and talents were legendary. After fourteen years of marriage, during which she bore fourteen children, Mumtaz Mahal died in childbirth in 1629. Shah Jahan was overcome with grief and committed himself to building for his wife the most extravagant and beautiful memorial ever created. It took 20,000 workers and artisans twenty-two years to complete the Taj Mahal.

The Taj is enormous, measuring 186 feet on each side, and rising to a height of 243 feet. But it is more notable for its beauty than its size. It is primarily constructed of white marble, set on a 30-foot square platform in a checkerboard design of black and white marble blocks. This in turn is set on another platform of rosy sandstone. From a distance, the white marble surface appears smooth and luminescent, especially when viewed in the glow of moonlight. But upon closer inspection, it can be seen that the Taj is not at all an unadorned expanse of marble. In fact, the entire surface is elaborately ornamented with *pietra dura* work, in which semi-precious gemstones are inlaid into the marble in various designs. Intricately decorated with carnelian, jasper, and other indigenous stones, the Taj could have been designed by a jeweler.

Shah Jahan had originally planned to build a companion to the Taj, a black marble mausoleum for himself which was to be joined to the Taj by a bridge. Before work on his tomb could begin, however, Shah Jahan was deposed and imprisoned by one of his sons, who decided his father's plan was too extravagant. Upon Shah Jahan's death, the new emperor ordered that a tomb for his father be built inside the Taj, in the octagonal room containing the sepulcher of the queen.

Recalling Facts

1. Mumtaz Mahal means
   - ☐ a. best of the palaces.
   - ☒ b. exalted of the palace.
   - ☐ c. wife of the emperor.

2. How long did it take to build the Taj Mahal?
   - ☐ a. 30 years
   - ☐ b. 14 years
   - ☒ c. 22 years

3. Each side of the Taj measures
   - ☒ a. 186 feet.
   - ☐ b. 243 feet.
   - ☐ c. 300 feet.

4. Carnelian and jasper are
   - ☐ a. architects.
   - ☐ b. sons of the emperor.
   - ☒ c. semi-precious stones.

5. The Taj is built mostly of
   - ☐ a. white marble.
   - ☒ b. rosy sandstone.
   - ☐ c. *pietra dura*.

Understanding the Passage

6. The Taj may be said to symbolize India because it
   - ☒ a. is the most representative work of architecture in the country.
   - ☐ b. is recognized by people everywhere.
   - ☐ c. was built with Indian materials.

7. The Taj was intended to be a
   - ☒ a. tomb for the royal couple.
   - ☐ b. temple for Arjuman Banu Begum.
   - ☐ c. tomb for Mumtaz Mahal.

8. Shah Jahan's son had his father entombed in the Taj
   - ☒ a. so he could be near his beloved wife for eternity.
   - ☐ b. because there was so much unused space inside.
   - ☐ c. to save the expense of building a new tomb.

9. Most people who visit the Taj
   - ☐ a. are inspired to write music or poetry.
   - ☐ b. don't believe it's a mausoleum.
   - ☒ c. are impressed by its beauty.

10. The Taj "could have been designed by a jeweler" because
    - ☐ a. jewelers use many of the same materials.
    - ☐ b. it was extremely expensive.
    - ☒ c. jewelers and artisans do similar work.

2   The Secretive Mr. Goddard

Of great importance to the future of space exploration was the work of the American physicist, Robert Goddard. While engaged in post-graduate work at Princeton University, Goddard had demonstrated in the laboratory that rocket propulsion would function in a vacuum; and in 1917 he received a grant of $5,000 from the Smithsonian Institution to continue his experiments. Under this grant the Smithsonian published the report of his theory and early experiments, *Method of Reaching Extreme Altitudes*. In 1918 he had successfully developed a solid-fuel ballistic rocket in which even the United States Army lost interest after the Armistice. Convinced that rockets would eventually permit travel into outer space, Goddard continued his research at Clark University. After the war, he sought to develop vehicles that could penetrate into the ionosphere. In 1926 he successfully launched a rocket propelled by gasoline and liquid oxygen, an experiment that ranks in fame with the Wright brothers' Kitty Hawk flights of 1903. With the help of Charles Lindbergh, after his dramatic solo trans-Atlantic flight, Goddard obtained a grant of $5,000 from Daniel Guggenheim and equipped a small laboratory in New Mexico where he built several rockets. In 1937, assisted by grants from the Guggenheim Foundation, he launched a rocket that reached an altitude of 9,000 feet.

Although not many people in the United States knew much about his work, a few had followed it as closely as his secretiveness allowed them to. Among them were members of the American Interplanetary Space Society, organized in 1930 and later renamed the American Rocket Society. With the coming of World War II, Goddard abandoned his field experiments; but the Navy employed him to help in developing liquid propellants for JATO, that is, jet-assisted takeoff for aircraft. When the Nazi "buzz" bombs of 1943 and the supersonic Vengeance missiles, the "V-2s" that rained on London during 1944 and early 1945, awakened the entire world to the potentialities of rockets as weapons, a good many physicists and military men studied his findings with attention.

By a twist of fate, Goddard, who was even more interested in astronautics than in weaponry, died in 1945, fourteen years before most of his countrymen acknowledged manned space exploration as feasible. The government recognized Goddard's basic contribution to space exploration by naming the new multimillion-dollar experimental station at Beltsville, Maryland, The Goddard Space Flight Center. Goddard paved the way for the advanced technological events in space taking place today.

Reading Time＿＿＿＿＿   *Comprehension Score*＿＿＿＿＿   *Words per Minute*＿＿＿＿＿

Recalling Facts

1. Robert Goddard did some post-graduate work at
   - ☐ a. Harvard College.
   - ☐ b. Yale University.
   - ☒ c. Princeton University.

2. The Smithsonian Institution awarded Goddard a grant of
   - ☒ a. $5,000.
   - ☐ b. $10,000.
   - ☐ c. $15,000.

3. In what year did Goddard develop a solid-fuel rocket?
   - ☐ a. 1914
   - ☐ b. 1918
   - ☒ c. 1926

4. Goddard built a small laboratory in
   - ☒ a. New Mexico.
   - ☐ b. Florida.
   - ☐ c. North Carolina.

5. The person who helped Goddard was
   - ☐ a. Amelia Earhart.
   - ☒ b. Charles Lindbergh.
   - ☐ c. Wilbur Wright.

Understanding the Passage

6. In laboratory work, Goddard proved that
   - ☒ a. rockets would function in the vacuum of outer space.
   - ☐ b. ballistic missiles were unsafe in warfare.
   - ☐ c. satellites could be launched with solid fuels.

7. The Kitty Hawk flights of the Wright brothers are mentioned to
   - ☐ a. prove that Goddard was not alone in rocket research.
   - ☒ b. illustrate the history of flight experimentation.
   - ☐ c. show the significance of Goddard's work.

8. The U.S. was not interested in Goddard's work because the
   - ☐ a. government was developing similar rockets.
   - ☐ b. war had just ended.
   - ☒ c. League of Nations disapproved of rocket research.

9. To honor Goddard, the government used his name for a
   - ☐ a. launch vehicle.
   - ☒ b. new type of rocket.
   - ☐ c. space center.

10. Goddard's published theories and experiments dealt with the
    - ☒ a. techniques of attaining great altitudes.
    - ☐ b. methods of launching interplanetary vehicles.
    - ☐ c. application of jets and rockets to peaceful purposes.

3 Disability Rights: Civil Rights

People with disabilities comprise a large but diverse segment of the population. It is estimated that over 35 million Americans have physical, mental, sensory, or other disabilities. Approximately half of these disabilities are "developmental," i.e., they occur prior to the individual's twenty-second birthday, often from genetic conditions, and are severe enough to affect three or more areas of development, such as mobility, communication, employment, etc. Most other disabilities are considered "adventitious," i.e., accidental or caused by outside forces.

Prior to this century, only a small percentage of people with disabilities survived for long. Medical treatment for such conditions as stroke, spinal cord injury, or polio was unavailable. People whose disabilities should not have inherently affected their life span were often so mistreated that they perished. These included the mentally retarded, the blind, and those with celebral palsy.

Advancements in medicine and social services have created a climate in which people with disabilities can expect to have such basic needs as food, shelter, and medical treatment met. Unfortunately, these basics are often all that is available. Civil liberties such as the right to vote, marry, get an education, and gain employment have historically been denied on the basis of disability.

In recent decades, the disability rights movement has been organized to combat these infringements of civil rights. Disabled people formed grass-roots coalitions to advocate their rights to integration and meaningful equality of opportunity. Congress responded by passing major legislation recognizing people with disabilities as a protected class under civil rights statutes. In the mid-1970s, critical legislation mandated access to education, public transportation, and public facilities, and prohibited employment discrimination by federal agencies or employers receiving federal funds.

Still today, people with disabilities must fight to live their lives independently. It is estimated that more than half of qualified Americans with disabilities are unemployed, and a majority of those who do work are underemployed. Approximately two-thirds live at or below the official poverty level.

Significant barriers, especially in transportation and public awareness, prevent disabled people from taking part in society. For example, while no longer prohibited by law from marrying, a person with no access to transportation is effectively excluded from community and social activities which might lead to the development of long-term relationships.

It will only be when public attitudes advance as far as laws have that disabled people will be fully able to take their rightful place in society.

Recalling Facts

1. The estimated number of disabled people in America is
   - ☒ a. 35 million.
   - ☐ b. 3.5 million.
   - ☐ c. 350,000.

2. A "developmental" disability
   - ☒ a. develops slowly over time.
   - ☐ b. affects the mental process.
   - ☐ c. occurs in youth and affects development.

3. An "adventitious" disability is
   - ☐ a. luckier than a developmental one.
   - ☐ b. caused by outside forces.
   - ☒ c. the least severe disability.

4. The number of disabled people who are unemployed is
   - ☐ a. one-half.
   - ☐ b. two-thirds.
   - ☒ c. three-fourths.

5. Civil rights laws of the 1970s addressed
   - ☐ a. marriage.
   - ☐ b. medicine and social services.
   - ☒ c. transportation and employment.

Understanding the Passage

6. Many disabled people used to die early because
   - ☐ a. a disability always destroys major bodily functions.
   - ☐ b. surgical techniques were not available.
   - ☒ c. they didn't receive medical care, food, and shelter.

7. The most important and successful advocates for disability rights have been
   - ☐ a. doctors and social workers.
   - ☐ b. members of Congress.
   - ☒ c. grassroots coalitions of disabled people.

8. There is high unemployment among disabled people because
   - ☒ a. current laws only address employers who get federal funding.
   - ☐ b. disabled people don't have good qualifications for work.
   - ☐ c. employers don't know the laws.

9. Disabled people still speak out for more civil rights because
   - ☐ a. they aren't grateful for the laws that were passed.
   - ☐ b. many aren't married yet.
   - ☒ c. they want greater equality of opportunity.

10. Equal opportunities for disabled people can best be achieved through
    - ☐ a. more federal legislation.
    - ☐ b. better jobs.
    - ☒ c. public awareness.

The Andersonville Horror

Besides the unhealthful, debilitating prison conditions, the Federal soldiers jailed at Andersonville, Georgia, during the Civil War had to contend with depredations by their own comrades who frequently stole food, clothing, and other valuables and who used violence to gain their ends. The Andersonville Raiders, a large, organized group of thieves and murderers, were the most notorious and dangerous predators. For nearly four months, the Raiders held sway inside the prison, and robberies and murders were daily occurrences. Finally, with the help of prison officials, the six ringleaders were captured. On July 11, 1864, after a quick trial by fellow inmates, they were hanged.

Because the prison was situated far from Union lines and because the dogs, used by the Confederates to track runaways, were efficient, escape from Andersonville was very difficult. Still, during the prison's existence, 329 prisoners escaped. Most of these slipped away while on work details outside the stockade.

When the emaciated survivors of Andersonville returned to their homes at the end of the war, there was widespread demand in the North for the punishment of those responsible for what many claimed were deliberately planned atrocities. Next to the assassination of President Abraham Lincoln, the Andersonville story was the most potent weapon in the arsenal of those who wished to impose a harsh reconstruction policy on the former Confederate States of America.

Despite numerous claims to the contrary, there was no conspiracy on the part of Confederate officials to deliberately exterminate the Federal soldiers confined at Andersonville. The horrors of Andersonville resulted principally from the breakdown of the Southern economy. Throughout the Civil War, the Confederacy suffered from three fundamental weaknesses that crippled its military operations and made the functioning of an efficient prisoner-of-war system virtually impossible. Because industrial output was inadequate for support of the armed forces, military prisons were extremely primitive in their construction, equipment, and maintenance. Second, the Quartermaster and Commissary Corps, for various reasons, were never able to properly clothe and feed the Confederate Army, let alone prisoners of war. Finally, after the first two years of war, rail and water transportation were so crippled that the movement of supplies to peripheral points in the Confederacy was frequently cut off. Andersonville was one of those peripheral points.

It is important to recall that almost as many Confederates died in Northern prison camps as the 30,218 Federals who expired in the Southern camps.

Recalling Facts

1. Approximately how many prisoners escaped from Andersonville?
   - ☐ a. 50
   - ☐ b. 125
   - ☒ c. 300

2. Escape from Andersonville was
   - ☐ a. commonplace.
   - ☐ b. easy.
   - ☒ c. difficult.

3. How long did the Andersonville Raiders remain active?
   - ☒ a. four months
   - ☐ b. one year
   - ☐ c. four years

4. The Andersonville Raiders were
   - ☐ a. Southern militia men.
   - ☒ b. Northern prisoners.
   - ☐ c. Confederate prison guards.

5. The horrors of Andersonville resulted primarily from the breakdown of the
   - ☐ a. United States judicial system.
   - ☒ b. Southern economy.
   - ☐ c. Northern resistance.

Understanding the Passage

6. The Andersonville Raiders were most notorious for their
   - ☐ a. capturing of escaped prisoners.
   - ☐ b. surprise raids on enemy camps.
   - ☒ c. killing and stealing within the prison.

7. The author suggests that
   - ☒ a. many prisoners made unsuccessful escape attempts from the prison.
   - ☐ b. Northern troops were better trained than Confederate troops.
   - ☐ c. the Confederate Army was well clothed and well fed.

8. From the information provided, we can assume that
   - ☒ a. Confederate officials conspired to exterminate Federal soldiers.
   - ☐ b. Andersonville suffered from severe shortages of supplies.
   - ☐ c. Andersonville was the center of Southern military operations.

9. The assassination of Abraham Lincoln is mentioned as an example of
   - ☐ a. distorted newspaper reporting.
   - ☒ b. an alleged Southern atrocity.
   - ☐ c. history repeating itself.

10. We can conclude that
    - ☒ a. conditions in Andersonville were worse than those in other Southern prisons.
    - ☐ b. the construction of Andersonville weakened the Confederate Army.
    - ☐ c. slavery was the primary cause of the Civil War.

5   Delinquent Youth

A major reason most experts today support concepts such as a youth services bureau is that traditional correctional practices fail to rehabilitate many delinquent youth. It has been estimated that as many as 70 percent of all youth who have been institutionalized are involved in new offenses following their release. Contemporary correctional institutions are usually isolated—geographically and socially—from the communities in which most of their inmates live. In addition, rehabilitative programs in the typical training school and reformatory focus on the individual delinquent rather than the environmental conditions that foster delinquency.

Finally, many institutions do not play an advocacy role on behalf of those committed to their care. They fail to do anything constructive about the back-home conditions—family, school, work—faced by the youthful inmates. As a result, institutionalization too often serves as a barrier to the successful return of former inmates to their communities.

Perhaps the most serious consequence of sending youth to large, centralized institutions is that too frequently these places serve as training grounds for criminal careers. The classic example of the adult offender who leaves prison more knowledgeable in the ways of crime than when he entered is no less true of the juvenile committed to a correctional facility. The failures of traditional correctional institutions, then, point to the need for the development of a full range of strategies and treatment techniques as alternatives to incarceration.

Most experts today favor the use of small, decentralized correctional programs located in, or close to, communities where the young offender lives. Halfway houses, all-day probation programs, vocational training and job placement services, remedial education activities, and street worker programs are among the community-based alternatives available for working with delinquent and potentially delinquent youth.

Over and above all the human factors cited, the case for community-based programs is further strengthened when cost is considered. While more progressive correctional programs such as all-day probation, remedial education, and job training can be costly, they are nowhere near as expensive as traditional incarceration. It has been estimated that it costs more to keep a youth in prison for a year than it would to send him to an expensive private college for the same period of time.

The continuing increase in juvenile delinquency rates only serves to heighten the drastic under-financing, the lack of adequately trained staff, and the severe shortage of manpower that characterize virtually every juvenile correction system.

Recalling Facts

1. According to this author, traditional correctional practices have
   - ☑ a. failed.
   - ☐ b. succeeded.
   - ☐ c. been ignored.

2. What percentage of youth are involved in new offenses after release from a correctional institution?
   - ☐ a. 30 percent
   - ☐ b. 50 percent
   - ☑ c. 70 percent

3. Contemporary correctional institutions are isolated
   - ☐ a. politically.
   - ☐ b. economically.
   - ☑ c. geographically.

4. The author calls institutionalization a
   - ☑ a. barrier.
   - ☐ b. crime.
   - ☐ c. sin.

5. Similar to an adult offender, a juvenile may learn
   - ☐ a. ways to leave prison.
   - ☑ b. new criminal techniques.
   - ☐ c. to take advantage of work programs.

Understanding the Passage

6. The author feels that rehabilitative programs should focus on the
   - ☐ a. individual delinquent.
   - ☑ b. conditions in which delinquents live.
   - ☐ c. attitudes of the community.

7. The author feels that halfway houses are
   - ☑ a. an insult to the intelligence of the criminal.
   - ☐ b. a logical solution to the problems of incarceration.
   - ☐ c. a danger to the community in which they are established.

8. This article implies that correctional institutions
   - ☐ a. are too limited in their treatment.
   - ☑ b. extend too far beyond their proposed range.
   - ☐ c. are too lax with disciplinary controls.

9. The content of this selection can best be described as
   - ☑ a. critical.
   - ☐ b. satirical.
   - ☐ c. narrative.

10. The main idea of this selection is that
    - ☐ a. all-day probation programs are less costly than imprisonment.
    - ☐ b. adult criminals leave prison with new skills.
    - ☑ c. a full range of alternative treatment techniques is needed.

6   Highways and Byways

Beautiful highways are safer because they provide restful and scenic views that reduce the monotony of driving. A beautiful and safety-enhancing feature of modern highways is a wide, landscaped median. A median reduces headlight glare from oncoming traffic. It provides a quieter, more pleasant ride with less distraction from surroundings. An outstanding example of a median that is useful and beautiful may be seen on parts of Interstate Highway 95 in Virginia. Native evergreens and flowering plants were wisely selected for landscaping these medians. In a few places where the traffic lanes are widely separated, rest parks are provided in the median area. The United States Interstate System is a 41,000-mile network of the finest roads in the world.

All roads require maintenance. Highway engineers have learned that maintenance of the traffic surface is impossible unless erosion is prevented on the road shoulders and backslopes. Experience has also shown that the best and most economical protection for roadsides is provided by living plants that also provide beauty along the highways. Public interest in beautiful roadways has been increasing through the past half-century. Interest reached a new peak during the 1965 White House Conference on Natural Beauty. This conference was a milestone in the history of American conservation. The day after the conference closed, the president sent to Congress proposals for legislation to require the use of a portion of federal highway funds for landscaping, beautification and recreation, and to eliminate outdoor advertising signs and junkyards along interstate highways.

The conference spawned a new level of activity in roadside beautification. But this new activity would not have been possible without the foundation provided by earlier research and action programs. One of the earliest studies of erosion control on roadsides was conducted in the Yazoo-Little Tallahatchie basin in Mississippi nearly fifty years ago. The Forest Service has also conducted education and demonstration programs to show lumbermen how to prevent erosion during logging operations.

Erosion control on roadsides is receiving major emphasis in small watersheds everywhere. An example is the Haynes Creek-Brushy Fork watershed in Georgia. The Soil Conservation Service assisted local people in stabilizing 52 miles of roadsides by planting grass, shrubs, and trees.

Highway departments in most states now employ landscape architects to plan and promote roadside erosion control and beautification. These actions have helped to protect our roadways, and have created pleasant and safer driving conditions.

Recalling Facts

1. Interstate Highway 95 runs through the state of
   - ☐ a. Maryland.
   - ☐ b. Mississippi.
   - ◪ c. Virginia.

2. The United States Interstate System consists of roads extending
   - ☐ a. 12,000 miles.
   - ☐ b. 27,000 miles.
   - ◪ c. 41,000 miles.

3. Most highway maintenance is concerned with
   - ☐ a. painting lines.
   - ◪ b. preventing erosion.
   - ☐ c. resurfacing roadbeds.

4. Public interest in beautiful roadways has been increasing for about
   - ☐ a. 20 years.
   - ☐ b. 40 years.
   - ◪ c. 50 years.

5. The White House Conference on Natural Beauty was held during the
   - ☐ a. 1940s.
   - ☐ b. 1950s.
   - ◪ c. 1960s.

Understanding the Passage

6. The White House Conference on Natural Beauty
   - ◪ a. created landscaped medians.
   - ☐ b. eliminated advertising signs along interstate highways.
   - ☐ c. raised highway tolls.

7. The Forest Service
   - ☐ a. taught people how to prevent erosion of the landscape.
   - ◪ b. planted trees to beautify interstate highways.
   - ☐ c. carried out federal legislation on beautifying highways.

8. The author's greatest concern is for
   - ☐ a. eliminating junkyards along major thoroughfares.
   - ☐ b. making highways safer at night.
   - ◪ c. preventing roadside erosion.

9. After the White House Conference on Natural Beauty had adjourned, the President
   - ☐ a. acted quickly on proposed legislation.
   - ◪ b. established the Soil Conservation Service.
   - ☐ c. gave the Supreme Court new law enforcement powers.

10. The White House Conference on Natural Beauty
   - ☐ a. meets every ten years.
   - ☐ b. based its decisions on research conducted earlier.
   - ◪ c. dealt with problems of highway construction.

7 Conservation

One basic concept of a classical conservation philosophy is the identity of uniqueness in the natural environment. Proper application of this concept includes biological and geological resources—both renewable and nonrenewable.

The establishment of Yellowstone Park a century ago was the first national step in implementing the concept. Here, a major land area was set aside in order to preserve unique natural features for the education and enjoyment of all people. The park has been protected in spite of great resource values known to exist within its boundaries such as gold, hydropower, and geothermal energy. The Everglades National Park is a subtropical, water-based ecology in its natural state. Other areas, such as the Alaska Wildlife Refuge, are protected and exempted even from the kind of access permitted in national parks. The federal government has set aside national parks, national monuments, and wildlife refuges. These wilderness areas are always expanding and improving.

In like fashion, mineral resource areas can be truly unique in their character and in their occurrence in the accessible part of the earth's crust. Famous mineral districts like Butte, Montana, Bingham Canyon, Utah, and Lead, South Dakota, are rare occurrences on a planetary basis. Unlike the unique vistas and wildlife domains, unusual mineral deposits serve the public good if they are recovered in a systematic way. In the long history of man, exploration and development of mineral resources at specific sites have been temporary operations. With proper planning before extraction is begun and proper restoration of the terrain after extraction, there need be little adverse environmental impact in acceptable tradeoff of resource values and multiple use of the total resource base.

The concept of multiple use and sustained yield were two guiding principles of the classical conservation philosophy expressed at the beginning of the 20th century. Conflicting uses and permanent damage to other potential resource values have been elements of recent debate and will remain as important subjects in a pluralistic society that requires both renewable and nonrenewable resources to maintain its health, welfare, and vigor. It is understandable now that economic values received highest priority during the developmental stage of our society. Today the American society is mature in an economic sense. Understandable pressures are increasing to preserve our dwindling acreage of the natural terrain, particularly on the public lands. These pressures arise from public awareness of environmental abuse by industry and consumers.

Recalling Facts

1. The Everglades National Park is an example of a
   - [X] a. water-based ecology.
   - ☐ b. nonrenewable resource.
   - ☐ c. temporary environment.

2. The author mentions mineral districts in the
   - ☐ a. West.
   - ☐ b. South.
   - [X] c. East.

3. Mineral deposits should be recovered
   - ☐ a. periodically.
   - ☐ b. regionally.
   - [X] c. systematically.

4. The concept of multiple use and sustained yield goes back to
   - ☐ a. 1900.
   - [X] b. 1920.
   - ☐ c. 1950.

5. The author feels that in an economic sense, the American society is
   - ☐ a. unrealistic.
   - ☐ b. childish.
   - [X] c. mature.

Understanding the Passage

6. The park with the tightest restrictions is
   - ☐ a. Yellowstone Park.
   - ☐ b. Everglades National Park.
   - [X] c. the Alaska Wildlife Refuge.

7. The author leads the reader to believe that
   - [X] a. biological and geological resources are not renewable.
   - ☐ b. national parks contain many untapped natural resources.
   - ☐ c. terrain cannot be restored after mineral extraction.

8. To make the point clear, the author uses
   - ☐ a. the technique of comparison and contrast.
   - [X] b. personal opinions supported by observable facts.
   - ☐ c. simple chronological order of events.

9. Butte, Bingham Canyon, and Lead are mentioned as examples of
   - ☐ a. famous wildlife domains.
   - ☐ b. delicate ecosystems.
   - [X] c. areas of superior mineral deposits.

10. The author feels that adverse environmental impact in mining
    - ☐ a. is a fact of life that is evident in every country.
    - ☐ b. illustrates an indifferent attitude toward the landscape.
    - [X] c. can be avoided through proper planning and restoration.

The Age of Abundance

For more than a century, the United States Department of Agriculture (USDA) has carried out an increasing variety of services. These services have been largely instrumental in making U.S. agriculture the most productive in the world. These services are well known. They include production and utilization research; conservation of soil, water, and timber; supervised credit to improve farming and family living; programs to extend electric power to almost all farms; and measures to support farm income and bring about needed adjustment in supply and demand.

The Department provides many services directly to all citizens of the United States and, in a sense, particularly to urban dwellers. These services, too, have hastened our entry into the age of abundance and steadily contribute to the "better life." For example, through many food distribution programs, the Department improves diets for the elderly, the unemployed, the disabled, children raised by one parent, and children in schools and institutions.

To assure clean, wholesome meat supplies, the USDA inspects all the meat and poultry products that are shipped across state lines. USDA grademarks on food help consumers get full value for their food dollars. New or improved foods, cotton, wool, leather, and other agricultural products come every year from USDA research laboratories. New marketing methods result in a higher food quality, less waste, and consumer savings, totaling millions of dollars annually.

USDA educational programs teach people to manage their incomes, buy wisely, prepare more nutritious meals, and to make proper use of credit.

Although the Department is not usually thought of as a health-protecting agency, it regularly makes contributions in this area. Penicillin, streptomycin, and other wonder drugs all have an agricultural background. Control of cancer, for example, may be aided by a world search now being carried out by the USDA to find plants containing substances that inhibit the disease.

USDA inspectors and cooperating customs officials keep a constant guard at U.S. ports and borders to prevent foreign crop and animal pests and diseases from becoming established in the United States.

USDA soil surveys and land use plans help public and private developers and engineers build on sound sites, thus saving taxpayers and individuals many millions of dollars every year. In the future, such services will be increasingly needed not only to meet the demands of a larger population, but also to continue the advance into better living, an important goal in the age of abundance.

Recalling Facts

1. The USDA inspects all meat and poultry products that are shipped
   - ☐ a. out of the country.
   - ☐ b. from Canada.
   - ☒ c. across state lines.

2. USDA research laboratories help to produce better qualities of
   - ☐ a. leather.
   - ☒ b. plastic.
   - ☐ c. glass.

3. New marketing methods developed by the USDA result in
   - ☐ a. higher costs.
   - ☒ b. less waste.
   - ☐ c. more stores.

4. USDA researchers are now working on a drug for the control of
   - ☐ a. malaria.
   - ☐ b. sleeping sickness.
   - ☒ c. cancer.

5. USDA inspectors work at U.S. ports and borders to prevent the influx of
   - ☐ a. marijuana.
   - ☒ b. diseases.
   - ☐ c. aliens.

Understanding the Passage

6. The article implies that the USDA
   - ☒ a. is a government agency.
   - ☐ b. extends its controls to foreign countries.
   - ☐ c. does intensive work in many American hospitals.

7. The USDA is discussed in this article as a
   - ☐ a. new corporation.
   - ☒ b. diversified organization.
   - ☐ c. private enterprise.

8. According to the author, the work of the USDA
   - ☐ a. has been limited by public apathy.
   - ☐ b. has been controversial in recent years.
   - ☒ c. is expanding continually.

9. Most people do not regard the USDA as
   - ☐ a. an agricultural agency.
   - ☐ b. a consumer-oriented agency.
   - ☒ c. a health-protecting agency.

10. From the information provided, the reader can assume that the USDA
    - ☒ a. is instrumental in the manufacture of penicillin.
    - ☐ b. has offices in most American cities.
    - ☐ c. has contributed research findings to the American space program.

9 A Place for Everything

Most people think their homes are safe, but frequently they are not. Statistics show a large proportion of accidents occur there. About one to two million people suffer from poisoning each year in the United States, and approximately 4,000 deaths result.

These poisonings result from swallowing or otherwise ingesting common materials such as kitchen and laundry cleaning aids, medicines, and cosmetics. Children often ingest garage and workshop items such as paints and varnishes and miscellaneous materials such as pesticides, moth balls, deodorizers, rust preventives, and typewriter cleaners. In some cases the poisonings result from inhaling fumes.

Home safety is everyone's job. There is an old saying: "A good home is a happy home." This also implies that a good home is clean, orderly, healthy, well managed, and safe. A safe home is one with a place for everything and everything in its place.

A home that met safety requirements in the past may not pass them today due to aging of the property and new standards. If a family has qualms about the safety of its home, every member of the family should evaluate the situation and take any corrective action needed immediately.

The various rooms in the house should be checked to determine the variety of hazardous materials present that could result in accidents or in death. Common potential poisons generally found in the home are medicine cabinet items such as prescription medications, cough syrups, aspirin, boric acid, camphorated oil, oil of wintergreen, rubbing alcohol and liniments, laxatives, antiseptics, and iodine.

Ingesting cosmetics such as hair removers, shaving creams and lotions, colognes and perfumes, nail polish and remover, cuticle remover, astringents, permanent wave solutions, suntan creams and oils, hair lotions, creams, and shampoos can also cause death.

Laundry and cleaning aids such as bleaches, drain cleaners, dyes, detergents, dry cleaners, floor and rug cleaners, ammonia, furniture polishes and waxes, and metal and jewelry cleaners can be lethal if swallowed.

Garage and workshop items such as paints and varnishes, shellacs, paint thinners and removers, insect poisons, auto polishes and waxes, plastic menders, gasoline, kerosene, certain chemicals used in photography, leather preservatives, moth balls and crystals, pesticides, deodorizers, rust preventives and removers, and typewriter cleaner can cause poisoning if consumed.

Volatile substances, which tend to vaporize and give off fumes or odors, can cause death. These materials may also be flammable, and for maximum safety should not be stored indoors.

Recalling Facts

1. About how many cases of poisoning occur each year?
   - ☐ a. 500,000
   - ☒ b. 1 to 2 million
   - ☐ c. 3 to 4 million

2. A home that was safe at one time may not be at a later time because
   - ☒ a. buildings age.
   - ☐ b. taxes increase.
   - ☐ c. people move.

3. Some common substances that are poisonous are also
   - ☐ a. expensive.
   - ☒ b. flammable.
   - ☐ c. explosive.

4. Poisons that the author mentions twice are
   - ☐ a. dyes.
   - ☐ b. perfumes.
   - ☒ c. moth balls.

5. Volatile substances should not be stored in
   - ☐ a. airtight cans.
   - ☐ b. cool places.
   - ☒ c. buildings.

Understanding the Passage

6. The author states that most people
   - ☒ a. think that potential poisons cannot be found in their homes.
   - ☐ b. store gasoline in open containers.
   - ☐ c. do not know how to treat victims of poisoning.

7. This article contains
   - ☐ a. the findings of a hospital study on poisons.
   - ☒ b. a list of common household poisons.
   - ☐ c. several reasons why children are attracted to poisons.

8. According to the author, aspirin
   - ☒ a. is one of the few safe medications in the medicine cabinet.
   - ☐ b. cannot be ingested with alcohol.
   - ☐ c. is a medicine that can be poisonous.

9. An old saying quoted by the author is:
   - ☒ a. A good home is a happy home.
   - ☐ b. A stitch in time saves nine.
   - ☐ c. Waste not, want not.

10. This article could have been titled
    - ☐ a. Garage and Workshop Poisons.
    - ☐ b. Living the Good Life.
    - ☒ c. An Ounce of Prevention.

10   Anne Bradstreet: the First American Woman Poet

Anne Bradstreet is credited as the first woman poet of the new world. This title is impressive; however, this accomplishment becomes even more remarkable when one examines her society. Bradstreet's works drew from her way of life, historically and religiously.

Bradstreet was born around 1612 in Northamptonshire to a wealthy family, and she enjoyed a fortunate childhood. Her father believed that all people should be educated; therefore, Bradstreet was taught all classical lessons. Around 1630 the Bradstreets, including the poet and her new husband, voyaged to the New World. Money and religion figured prominently as motives for this adventure. In Andover, Massachusetts, Bradstreet was successful in her accomplishments, such as managing a relatively impressive home, mothering eight children, maintaining the Puritan role of an obedient wife, and writing poetry. Bradstreet died on September 16, 1672, but her poetry keeps her name alive today as many people read and appreciate her works of literature.

Before one can fully comprehend Bradstreet's poems, it is important that her Puritan beliefs are understood. Puritanism is a religion which originated in England during the reign of Henry VIII after the king split away from the Catholic Church and developed the Church of England. The Puritans were extreme and wished to abolish any hint of Catholicism. The extremity of their beliefs earned the Puritans much persecution, and many fled to the New World in hopes of freedom.

One Puritan belief was predestination, which states that God has decided, before a person's birth, whether he or she will find eternal damnation or salvation. God's chosen people, then, must live moral lives and guide others to understand God's superiority. Bradstreet followed these basic principles, which enhanced her gift, but probably also hindered complete development of her talent. This was due to the scorn that an over-ambitious Puritan woman could expect to receive. However, when her first set of works, *The Tenth Muse Lately Sprung Up in America*, was published in 1650, Bradstreet received great praise. Many of Bradstreet's poems honestly reflect her thoughts on domestic and religious life. Bradstreet admitted that she sometimes doubted her faith and was not a perfect Puritan. When her "heart rose" against the faith, she had to put her trust in God. This is reflected in many poems containing themes such as gratitude, love, and the value of earthly possessions as opposed to faith. Two famous poems are "Upon the Burning of our House July 10th, 1666," and "The Flesh and the Spirit." Anne Bradstreet continues to be appreciated for her ability to write beautiful poetry and her eagerness to share her true emotions.

Recalling Facts

1. Who was the first female American poet?
   - ☐ a. Emily Dickinson
   - ☒ b. Anne Bradstreet
   - ☐ c. Adrienne Rich

2. The person most responsible for Bradstreet's education was her
   - ☒ a. father.
   - ☐ b. teacher.
   - ☐ c. mother.

3. The Bradstreets settled in
   - ☐ a. Plymouth, Massachusetts.
   - ☒ b. Andover, Massachusetts.
   - ☐ c. Roanoke, Virginia.

4. Where did the Puritan religion originate?
   - ☒ a. America
   - ☐ b. France
   - ☐ c. England

5. When was Bradstreet's first set of works published?
   - ☒ a. 1650
   - ☐ b. 1672
   - ☐ c. 1630

Understanding the Passage

6. The two things that caused the Bradstreets to flee to the new world were
   - ☐ a. disease and money.
   - ☒ b. religion and fear of the king.
   - ☐ c. money and religion.

7. Predestination stated that God decided in advance
   - ☒ a. whether someone would be damned or saved.
   - ☐ b. whether the Bradstreets would safely arrive at the New World.
   - ☐ c. who would be the next king of England.

8. Puritanism sometimes hindered Bradstreet's writing because
   - ☐ a. she was too busy worshipping to write.
   - ☒ b. she feared reprisal for appearing ambitious and bold.
   - ☐ c. her husband forbade poetry in the house.

9. One thing that makes Bradstreet's poetry so beautiful and touching is
   - ☒ a. her honesty in explaining her emotions and feelings.
   - ☐ b. her exquisite use of words.
   - ☐ c. the fact that she was not allowed to write.

10. Bradstreet's themes included
    - ☐ a. self-determination and greed.
    - ☐ b. lack of confidence and trust.
    - ☒ c. gratitude and love.

11   Evaluation without Intimidation

Evaluating employee performance is a key area of management skills. The challenge is to give the employees an accurate picture of their accomplishments, and of the areas in which they need to improve. Both are important: accomplishments because they give the employee a sense of pride in the work and a basis on which to build future achievements, and areas for improvement, because they give the employee some goals to reach for.

Often, employees fear that the evaluation will be a negative experience. This fear alone can engender defensiveness and tension which results in a self-fulfilling prophecy. The supervisor must take pains to alleviate the employee's fear and make the evaluation a participatory event. An employee who contributes ideas to his or her evaluation will be much more likely to ● agree with the outcome and be willing to follow the recommendations.

The employer must always bear in mind that the sole legitimate domain of an employee appraisal system is to improve employee performance. While areas needing improvement must be reviewed, this should always be done in the spirit of discovering goals the employee can work toward. This holds true for reviewing successes as well. While praise for past achievements may be used as a reward, to engender loyalty, or for other reasons, at the time of the evaluation, the primary reason to look at the person's ● successes is to determine areas in which he/she can continue to excel.

Perhaps the most effective way to make the evaluation a participatory event is to ask the employee to come prepared to the meeting. The employer and employee each should carefully review the job description prior to the evaluation meeting and should make notes on areas in which the employee had difficulty or has made a contribution. It is important that these notes be specific: "Does a good job" is not nearly as meaningful as "Increased productivity by 35%."

Both parties should also draw up a short list of goals for the employee ● to achieve during the next evaluation period. Ideally, these goals should build upon the known strengths and successes of the employee. However, areas needing improvement must also be addressed.

At the evaluation meeting, the employer must establish a positive and comfortable mood. The employee should be invited to review his or her lists first. Almost always, the employee's notes will be very similar to what the employer has written. If the employer simply verifies what the employee has said, the employee will be much less anxious about the procedure, and much more likely to work toward the goals.

Recalling Facts

1. Employees being evaluated often feel
   - ☐ a. proud.
   - ☒ b. fearful and anxious.
   - ☐ c. like quitting.

2. Evaluations should focus on
   - ☐ a. accomplishments.
   - ☐ b. areas needing improvement.
   - ☒ c. both of these.

3. One way to alleviate employee anxiety is to
   - ☐ a. ask the employee to contribute ideas.
   - ☐ b. serve coffee at the meeting.
   - ☒ c. set easy goals.

4. The sole legitimate domain of evaluations is to
   - ☐ a. tell employees how well they've done.
   - ☐ b. gain participation in the process.
   - ☒ c. improve employee performance.

5. The mood of the evaluation meeting should be
   - ☐ a. positive and comfortable.
   - ☒ b. polite but formal.
   - ☐ c. defensive.

Understanding the Passage

6. Evaluations are often a negative experience because the
   - ☐ a. employer doesn't have clear goals.
   - ☒ b. employee is tense, and the employer doesn't alleviate this.
   - ☐ c. employee has done a bad job.

7. Employees can better improve their performance if they
   - ☐ a. are praised for every success.
   - ☐ b. increase productivity.
   - ☒ c. agree with the goals that are set.

8. The key to participatory evaluation is that both parties
   - ☐ a. get to talk.
   - ☒ b. contribute ideas and agree on the outcome.
   - ☐ c. are comfortable in the setting.

9. The best way to tell if an evaluation was successful is to
   - ☐ a. ask the employee if he or she was tense during the meeting.
   - ☐ b. ask the employee if he or she agreed with the recommendations.
   - ☒ c. monitor the employee's future performance to see if the goals are met.

10. Evaluations should reflect the job description because
    - ☒ a. the job description relates to areas of performance.
    - ☐ b. this helps the employer remember what the employee did all year.
    - ☐ c. the employer and employee will have the same documentation.

The Unknown Land

To the seamen of the 18th century who skirted its ice-choked seas in their wooden vessels, Antarctica was known as "Terra Australis Incognito"—the unknown land of the South. Who first saw Antarctic lands is uncertain. On November 17, 1820, Nathaniel Palmer, captain of a Connecticut fur-sealing vessel, almost certainly sighted the continent and in his logbook mentioned seeing land.

On the first official United States government expedition to Antarctica in 1838, Navy Lieutenant Charles Wilkes found erratic blocks of continental-type rocks—granite and sandstone. These rocks, carried far northward by floating icebergs, pointed to the existence of a large south polar continent. Today part of Antarctica is called Wilkes Land in his honor.

The pioneering explorations of the continent itself were begun in 1901 by Sir Ernest Shackleton, Captain Robert F. Scott, Roald Amundsen, Sir Douglas Mawson, and many others. Many thrilling stories have been told about this heroic age of Antarctic discovery.

Americans did not become prominent in Antarctic exploration until later. Rear Admiral Richard E. Byrd was the first to use the airplane, tractor, and radio extensively on the continent, and his expedition in 1928–30 included the first flight over the South Pole. Another American aviator, Lincoln Ellsworth, flew across the continent in 1935 and surveyed from the air the area known as the American Highland.

Expeditions using modern technology inevitably became too expensive for private parties to undertake. The U.S. government officially sponsored the Antarctic Service Expedition to the Antarctic Peninsula and Ross Sea areas in the late 1930s, and also the massive aerial photographic mission, Operation Highjump, by the U.S. Navy under Admiral Byrd in 1946–47. These expeditions were followed the next season by Operation Windmill to establish ground control for map compilation and by the Ronne Antarctic Research Expedition in the southern Antarctic Peninsula in 1947. The United States participated in many exploratory and scientific programs carried out during and since the International Geophysical year of 1957–58.

The continent gradually became a vast experiment in international scientific cooperation. In December 1959, the Antarctic Treaty was signed by twelve countries who agreed to make no territorial claims for the duration of the thirty-year treaty, to use the continent for peaceful purposes only, to open the operations of each country to inspection by any other nation, and to preserve and conserve Antarctic resources. These agreements have led to cooperation among the countries involved and advancements in scientific research.

Recalling Facts

1. When Nathaniel Palmer
   spotted Antarctica, he was
   looking for
   ☑ a. whales.
   ☐ b. seals.
   ☐ c. penguins.

2. The first official United States
   government expedition to
   Antarctica occurred during the
   late
   ☑ a. 1830s.
   ☐ b. 1860s.
   ☐ c. 1890s.

3. How many countries signed
   the Antarctic Treaty?
   ☐ a. four
   ☐ b. six
   ☑ c. twelve

4. The first person to use a
   tractor in Antarctica was
   ☐ a. Amundsen.
   ☑ b. Ellsworth.
   ☐ c. Byrd.

5. Operation Highjump was
   concerned with
   ☐ a. climbing mountains.
   ☐ b. taking photographs.
   ☑ c. parachuting supplies.

Understanding the Passage

6. The author suggests that Ernest
   Shackleton and Robert Scott
   ☑ a. discovered Antarctica
       by accident.
   ☐ b. did not achieve fame in
       their lifetimes.
   ☐ c. were from European countries.

7. Individual explorations to
   Antarctica succumbed to
   government explorations because
   ☐ a. governments were better
       equipped for research.
   ☐ b. the expense became prohibitive.
   ☑ c. most countries discouraged
       private explorations.

8. Operation Windmill resulted in
   ☐ a. inexpensive electricity for
       Antarctic bases.
   ☑ b. a mapping of the Antarctic
       continent.
   ☐ c. peace agreements between
       the United States and Russia.

9. In Antarctica, no country is allowed to
   ☐ a. conduct research on the
       polar icecap.
   ☐ b. inspect the operations of
       other countries.
   ☑ c. test nuclear devices.

10. We can conclude from this
    selection that
    ☑ a. Antarctica no longer is considered
        "Terra Australis Incognito."
    ☐ b. explorations to Antarctica have
        been halted temporarily.
    ☐ c. Antarctica cannot support
        life on a year-round basis.

13 The Drinker's Dilemma

Prolonged and excessive use of alcohol can seriously undermine an individual's health. Physical deterioration occurs because large quantities of alcohol can directly damage body tissue and indirectly cause malnutrition. Nutritional deficiencies can result for several reasons. Alcohol contains empty calories and has no significant nutritive value. When consumed in substantial amounts, alcohol curbs one's appetite for more wholesome foods. Excessive alcohol intake can interfere with the proper digestion and absorption of food. Therefore, even the heavy drinker who does eat a well-balanced diet is deprived of some essential nutrients. Maintenance of a drinking habit can deplete economic resources otherwise available for buying good, wholesome food. Malnutrition itself further reduces the body's ability to utilize the nutrients consumed. The results of damaged tissue and malnutrition can be brain injury, heart disease, diabetes, ulcers, cirrhosis or cancer of the liver, and weakened muscle tissue. Untreated alcoholism can reduce one's life span by ten to twelve years.

Heavy alcohol consumption also affects the body's usage of other drugs and medications. The dosages required by excessive drinkers may differ from those required by normal drinkers or non-drinkers. Serious consequences can be incurred unless the prescribing physician is aware of the patient's drinking habits.

Sudden death may result from excessive drinking. It might occur when the individual has ingested such a large amount of alcohol that the brain center controlling breathing and heart action is adversely affected, or when taking some other drugs, particularly sleep preparations, along with alcohol. Death, as a result of excessive drinking, can come during an automobile accident, since over half of all fatal traffic accidents involve the use of alcohol. Many self-inflicted deaths, as well as homicides, involve the use of alcohol.

It is important to remember that alcohol is a drug that is potentially addictive. Once the user is hooked on alcohol, withdrawal symptoms occur when it is not sufficiently available to body cells. At the onset of developing alcohol addiction, these symptoms may be relatively mild and include hand tremors, anxiety, nausea, and sweating. As dependency increases, so does the severity of the withdrawal syndrome and the need for medical assistance to cope with it.

In 1956, the American Medical Association supported the growing acceptance of alcoholism as an illness, falling under the treatment jurisdiction of the medical profession. Since then, the medical resources for problems of acute and chronic intoxication have increased and improved.

*Reading Time*_____ *Comprehension Score*_____ *Words per Minute*_____

Recalling Facts

1. Untreated alcoholism can reduce a person's life by
   - ☐ a. 5 years.
   - ☒ b. 12 years.
   - ☐ c. 22 years.

2. The article points out that heavy drinking can cause
   - ☐ a. arthritis.
   - ☒ b. muscle debility.
   - ☐ c. blindness.

3. What fraction of all fatal traffic accidents results from the abuse of alcohol?
   - ☐ a. one-quarter
   - ☐ b. one-half
   - ☒ c. two-thirds

4. The author refers to alcohol as a
   - ☒ a. drug.
   - ☐ b. medicinal substance.
   - ☐ c. high calorie beverage.

5. A heavy drinker may suffer from
   - ☐ a. indigestion.
   - ☒ b. malnutrition.
   - ☐ c. excessive thirst.

Understanding the Passage

6. This selection is concerned mostly with the
   - ☒ a. long-term drinker.
   - ☐ b. person who drinks on a dare.
   - ☐ c. person who drinks for the first time.

7. A person who drinks to excess must show caution in
   - ☐ a. having X-rays.
   - ☐ b. engaging in exercise.
   - ☒ c. taking drugs.

8. The author develops a correlation between alcohol
   - ☐ a. use and theft.
   - ☐ b. absorption and insomnia.
   - ☒ c. addiction and withdrawal symptoms.

9. In the middle 1950s, the American Medical Association
   - ☐ a. proved that alcoholism is an act of free choice.
   - ☐ b. concluded that heredity influenced alcoholism.
   - ☒ c. accepted alcoholism as an illness.

10. The author suggests that
   - ☐ a. the American Medical Association once condoned drinking.
   - ☒ b. drinking alcohol can be an expensive habit.
   - ☐ c. eating a well-balanced diet enables a person to drink more.

Hills and Curves

Highway engineers have three objectives in planning and constructing today's heavily traveled transportation arteries. The objectives are greater safety, reduced maintenance costs, and general roadside attractiveness. Natural beauty contributes strongly to this threefold objective.

Highway architects have learned to fit the highway to the landscape by disturbing the natural landscape as little as possible. A highway that fits naturally into its surroundings gives the user the feeling that he is a part of the land. Interstate Highway 24, northwest of Chattanooga, Tennessee, is a beautiful highway designed in such a way as to give the traveler a feeling of fitting into the hills while enjoying a panoramic view of the countryside. Landscape architects have learned to use plantings to outline hills and curves and introduce vertical and horizontal dimensions that tend to make driving safer.

Roadway designers need hundreds of bits of specific information for every mile of roadway. For example, they must have accurate information about the soil over which their road will pass. Soil surveys are used by highway planners in identifying problem areas along the route. They also use soil surveys to select locations that have beauty as well as utility. In this way, soil surveys reduce the number of soil borings, cut costs, and speed up highway planning.

From soil surveys, the design engineer may also secure information about physical and chemical characteristics of the soil and its suitability for various uses. Physical characteristics of the soil include texture, structure, and arrangement of layers.

Research scientists studying the physical and mechanical properties have learned that some soil material is unsuitable for roadways because it shrinks and swells too much. They have learned that permeable material overlying dense clay or shale is susceptible to slippage. Cuts through hills must be designed to avoid this danger.

Highway designers use soil information to select suitable sources of surface soil and to locate rest and recreation areas. Roadside rest areas present many unique problems because they must be accessible, functional, and beautiful. The soil and its grass cover must be able to withstand heavy pedestrian traffic. The soil must contain plant nutrients and have physical characteristics that prevent it from becoming soft and spongy during the rainy periods. Planting and maintaining grass, trees, and shrubs on highways is difficult. Such work requires much knowledge and experience because soil and site conditions along highways vary more than natural conditions in the surrounding area.

Recalling Facts

1. How many objectives are considered in planning and constructing highways?
   - ☐ a. two
   - ☑ b. three
   - ☐ c. four

2. The author discusses Interstate Highway 24 in the state of
   - ☐ a. Alabama.
   - ☐ b. Connecticut.
   - ☑ c. Tennessee.

3. Interstate Highway 24 runs
   - ☐ a. along a river.
   - ☑ b. through the hills.
   - ☐ c. over swamplands.

4. Highway designers need accurate information about
   - ☐ a. climate.
   - ☑ b. soil.
   - ☐ c. vegetation.

5. Roadway designers are careful not to plan rest areas where
   - ☐ a. traffic is very heavy.
   - ☐ b. signs may be required at a later time.
   - ☑ c. the ground may become muddy.

Understanding the Passage

6. This article is primarily about
   - ☐ a. traffic control on major highways.
   - ☐ b. building secondary roads.
   - ☑ c. making roads safe and attractive.

7. Interstate Highway 24 is cited as an example of a
   - ☐ a. major artery that blends in with the environment.
   - ☐ b. thoroughfare with innovative rest areas.
   - ☑ c. superhighway with landscaped medians.

8. Roads cannot be made of permeable materials overlying shale because the surface would
   - ☑ a. be too dense.
   - ☐ b. be unstable.
   - ☐ c. discolor.

9. The author implies that
   - ☐ a. making soil borings is a slow process.
   - ☑ b. soil borings are not as accurate as soil samples.
   - ☐ c. soil borings are often made after a highway is completed.

10. The reader can conclude that
    - ☑ a. highway safety can be improved through proper construction methods.
    - ☐ b. most highways require repairs after every five years of use.
    - ☐ c. the soil used for most highways is a mixture of sand and loam.

15   More Rare Than Rubies

There was a time when the word "prospector" conjured up visions of whiskery desert rats toting pickaxes and shambling with their mules out of a thousand Western novels toward a thousand cinematic sunsets.

No more. Prospecting has joined the space age. It hasn't happened in a flash. Over the years, mineral companies have analyzed water flowing in mountain streams for clues to ore bodies. Electrical and magnetic prospecting devices used in combination with geochemical analyses and field studies have led the mineral industry to a variety of ore deposits.

Recent changes have been toward greater sophistication. Today's tools are infrared cameras and mercury vapor detectors, computers and helicopters. And in addition, modern prospectors scrutinize the treetops, study sound waves, and observe plant life.

What's behind the transformation? It all began as a kind of scientific detective case. The culprit in this caper was technological society. Like a glutton on a binge, it was eating up the rare heavy metals—tin, antimony, mercury, bismuth, nickel, tantalum, platinum, silver, and gold. With precious reserves dwindling ominously, the U.S. Geological Survey, an arm of the Department of the Interior, began field-testing techniques that may aid in uncovering additional mineral resources.

The government acted because these rare metals are vitally necessary to sophisticated 20th century technology. Each of them has a long list of uses, and many of them are absolutely indispensable.

Nickel is added to steel wherever great strength and corrosion resistance are needed. Mercury, used in scientific apparatus, is also vital to the electronics industry for such components as rectifiers and switches.

Platinum, too, is used in electronics (for contact points), while tin goes into such important products as solder. Antimony plays a part in rubber production, and gold and silver aren't limited to baubles.

Photography depends on silver compounds, and the United States alone annually consumes over thirty million ounces of silver for electronic parts like telephone relays.

Without gold (for semiconductors, connectors, and printed circuits), computers wouldn't think so fast. A shortage of these metals, and others like them, would create a serious problem for society.

For the Survey's geologist-sleuths, it was a tough assignment: how to track down new deposits of the vital metals? By now, few ore deposits marked by surface outcrops are undiscovered. The deposits that space-age prospectors have to search out are hidden under tons of rock and earth.

Recalling Facts

1. The United States Geological Survey is a branch of which government department?
   - ☐ a. Agriculture
   - ☐ b. Commerce
   - ☒ c. Interior

2. The metal added to steel for greater strength is
   - ☒ a. nickel.
   - ☐ b. platinum.
   - ☐ c. bismuth.

3. The electronics industry is greatly dependent upon
   - ☐ a. nickel.
   - ☒ b. mercury.
   - ☐ c. antimony.

4. How many ounces of silver does the United States consume annually for electronics?
   - ☐ a. 10 million
   - ☐ b. 20 million
   - ☒ c. 30 million

5. Who initiated a drive to ensure continued supplies of rare metals?
   - ☐ a. mineral companies
   - ☐ b. the government
   - ☒ c. electronics companies

Understanding the Passage

6. This article is primarily about
   - ☐ a. the mining of precious metals.
   - ☐ b. prospecting for precious metals.
   - ☒ c. the need for precious metals.

7. The phrase "like a glutton on a binge, it was eating up . . . metals" is
   - ☐ a. literal language.
   - ☐ b. figurative language.
   - ☒ c. scientific description.

8. The function of the United States Geological Survey is to
   - ☒ a. uncover new sources of minerals.
   - ☐ b. develop new laboratory technology to conserve rare metals.
   - ☐ c. find territory which has never been explored for minerals.

9. The author implies that gold and silver are used
   - ☐ a. primarily by the jewelry industry.
   - ☒ b. in the manufacture of many products.
   - ☐ c. in smaller quantities than other metals.

10. We can conclude that
    - ☒ a. new sources of heavy metals will be found.
    - ☐ b. used metals must be recycled if supplies are to last.
    - ☐ c. industry must find substitute metals which are more common.

16 The Magical Food

To the true connoisseur, chocolate is not merely a food; it is almost an emotional experience. Consider the names of just a few American companies: Chocolate Fantasy, Chocolate Heaven, Aphrodite's Confections of Love. More than 1,000 years ago, the Mayans of Central America used cocoa beans as a unit of legal tender, and the unsweetened beverage they brewed from these was considered to have mystical properties.

When the Aztecs conquered the Mayans, they enforced a tribute of cocoa beans as a type of taxation. They continued to use the beans as currency, and also brewed a powerful beverage from them. The use of cocoa spread throughout the New World, and it was transported back to the Old World by Christopher Columbus. The Spanish aristocracy developed new methods of brewing cocoa, sometimes adding vanilla and cinnamon, but sometimes adding hot chili peppers! Perhaps the Spaniards too ascribed magical powers to the beverage, since they kept it a secret for almost one hundred years. Around this same time, sugar began to be added to the brew, and hot cocoa as we know it today was born.

By the seventeenth century, chocolate had gained a reputation as an aphrodisiac. Casanova himself partook of cocoa before embarking on his amorous adventures, and considered the potion to be partially responsible for his successful seductions. In 1775, Swedish botanist Carolus Linnaeus, in his classification of plants, designated the cocoa tree *Theobroma*, a Greek word meaning "food of the gods." Whether or not Linnaeus was aware of the opinions of Casanova on the matter, he clearly regarded chocolate as more than merely flavorful.

Phenylethylamine, a naturally occurring chemical stimulant, has been discovered to be the secret ingredient of chocolate. Phenylethylamine is released by the human brain when people become infatuated; conversely, phenylethylamine levels drop when people end relationships. It is hypothesized that those who overindulge in chocolate at the termination of a love affair are merely seeking to compensate for this lower level of stimulation by ingesting the phenylethylamine in chocolate.

If additional justification for chocolate consumption is needed, the epicure can take comfort in nutritional information provided by the Chocolate Manufacturers' Association of America, which has determined that chocolate contains protein, riboflavin, iron, and other nutrients. One can always overlook the two major nutrients in chocolate: carbohydrates and fats.

Recalling Facts

1. The first culture to use chocolate as money was the
   - ☐ a. Aztec.
   - ☐ b. Mayan.
   - ☒ c. Spanish.

2. The botanical name of the cocoa plant is
   - ☐ a. *Theobroma.*
   - ☐ b. *Theologica.*
   - ☒ c. *Linnaeus.*

3. Cocoa was brought to Europe by
   - ☐ a. the Aztecs.
   - ☐ b. Spanish explorers.
   - ☒ c. Columbus.

4. Phenylethylamine occurs in chocolate and
   - ☐ a. other plants.
   - ☐ b. nutrients.
   - ☒ c. the human brain.

5. Chocolate's primary nutrients are
   - ☐ a. fats and carbohydrates.
   - ☒ b. phenylethylamine and protein.
   - ☐ c. iron and riboflavin.

Understanding the Passage

6. The value placed on chocolate by some cultures is evidenced by
   - ☐ a. the number of people who love it.
   - ☐ b. its nutritional level.
   - ☒ c. its use as currency.

7. The article suggests that cocoa as a beverage
   - ☐ a. was always popular.
   - ☒ b. has taken many different forms and flavors.
   - ☐ c. used to be expensive.

8. The writer implies that the Chocolate Manufacturers' information
   - ☐ a. is valid and reliable.
   - ☒ b. may be biased.
   - ☐ c. is a good reason to eat chocolate.

9. People who eat chocolate when a love affair ends
   - ☒ a. may be trying to restore a level of stimulation.
   - ☐ b. don't care if they get fat.
   - ☐ c. need the nutrition in candy.

10. Among chocolate's supposedly magical powers is that it
    - ☐ a. has good nutrition and great flavor.
    - ☒ b. increases sexual desire and prowess.
    - ☐ c. was eaten by Aztec gods.

17 Make, Model, and Year

Automotive paint is such a common substance that the motoring public is often unaware that small chips can be very valuable clues in hit-and-run investigations.

Paint transfer occurs in many collisions involving vehicles. At the scene of a hit-and-run accident, for example, police personnel often collect paint samples from a struck vehicle, from related debris, or from the clothing of a struck pedestrian, either in smear form or as actual chips.

Laboratory technicians are then asked to examine the paint samples and to classify or individualize them. A classification helps to determine the probable make, model, and year of the vehicle involved and is useful in the early stages of an investigation. An individualization serves to establish that the paint came from a particular vehicle and is a more specific characterization. The simplest methods of paint characterization involve the microscopic examination of color, surface texture, surface markings and layer structure, and the matching of broken edges.

The Law Enforcement Standards Laboratory (LESL), as part of its effort to develop performance standards and reference materials for the National Institute of Law Enforcement and Criminal Justice, established an auto paint reference collection and data supplement for use by state and local forensic science laboratories.

In 1973, LESL conducted a study of the availability of standard reference collections and their relative importance to forensic laboratories. The study showed that an automotive paint reference collection was of prime importance. LESL, with the cooperation of auto manufacturers and their paint suppliers, has been filling this need.

The first reference collection consisted of samples of about 140 paint colors used on 1974 domestic passenger vehicles. All the color samples in the collection were prepared from actual paint patches. The paint suppliers applied the paint to primed panels. Samples, about one inch square, were then cut, and each sample was placed in a hinged plastic slide holder. The holders were placed in special plastic slide containers that were assembled in three-ring binders. The samples can be removed from the hinged holders for ease in visual or microscopic examination.

The samples are arranged in the collection according to their colors. However, the flexibility of the system permits the user to organize the samples in any way he wishes.

These reference sets are distributed to qualified forensic laboratories throughout the nation.

Since the initial steps were taken, many accidents have been solved by what may have once looked like insignificant evidence.

Recalling Facts

1. The simplest method of paint characterization involves
   - ☑ a. microscopic examination.
   - ☐ b. chemical analysis.
   - ☐ c. photoelectric scanning.

2. The first reference collection of LESL consisted of about
   - ☐ a. 50 paint colors.
   - ☐ b. 90 paint colors.
   - ☑ c. 140 paint colors.

3. The size of each color sample was
   - ☑ a. one inch square.
   - ☐ b. three inches square.
   - ☐ c. six inches square.

4. LESL paint samples were stored in
   - ☐ a. rotary files.
   - ☐ b. microfilm files.
   - ☑ c. three-ring binders.

5. All the paint samples in the first collection were used on
   - ☐ a. 1970 cars.
   - ☐ b. 1972 cars.
   - ☑ c. 1974 cars.

Understanding the Passage

6. Which one of the following cars is not represented in the first collection?
   - ☐ a. Chevrolet
   - ☑ b. Volkswagen
   - ☐ c. Plymouth

7. According to the article, LESL
   - ☑ a. investigates car accidents.
   - ☐ b. prosecutes people who are guilty of reckless driving.
   - ☐ c. develops performance standards for law enforcement agencies.

8. The 1973 LESL study of available paint references showed that
   - ☐ a. a reference library of automobile paints was badly needed.
   - ☐ b. many car manufacturers used the same paint colors.
   - ☑ c. most police departments needed a forensic laboratory.

9. The author states that
   - ☑ a. automobile paint is the most durable paint available.
   - ☐ b. bright sunlight sometimes alters the color of paint.
   - ☐ c. many reference sets were made and distributed.

10. We can conclude that LESL
    - ☑ a. is a branch of the Department of Justice.
    - ☐ b. is financed by car manufacturers.
    - ☐ c. dictates color standards to car makers.

18   Fundraising Without Funds

A familiar adage says "It takes money to make money." In the financial investment world, this is doubtless accurate. Those investors who multiply their wealth are generally those with sufficient initial capital to diversify.

Usually the adage also applies to fundraising. Most development officers in non-profit corporations expect that initial outlays of money are a necessary prerequisite to making money. For example, to solicit individual contributions, the development officer must pay for printing, labeling, sorting, and mailing each letter of request.

The same principle holds true for special events fundraising. While gala celebrations or benefit performances may be attractive events which will increase an organization's visibility, they are very costly to produce and may net little profit.

There are two fundraisers, however, which a non-profit organization can put on at little cost: raffles and yard sales. These events may not provide the same visibility or reputation for elegance as a gala, but they are an effective way to raise money on a shoestring budget, and if well organized, can be lots of fun for the participants.

Organizing a raffle is extremely easy, whether you have a few or many volunteers. The feature which makes raffles so easy is that the time frame can be expanded as needed to get everything done.

The first thing to do is to ask individuals and businesses to make donations, which may be tax-deductible, of goods or services. Then have tickets printed, preferably listing the prizes right on the tickets. Many printers will donate their services for this work; even if they don't, the printing is not a costly item. All that's left to do is to sell the tickets and hold a drawing.

Yard sales are perhaps more difficult to organize, but well worth the effort. Because they need to take place on a specific date, and much of the work is last-minute set-up, it is best to have a large group of volunteers for this event. The organizer should assign responsibility for collecting and pricing donations, advertising, setting up the display, and staffing the actual sale.

Organizers are often amazed at how lucrative a yard sale can be, especially if they advertise enough to attract the collectors, dealers, and other "professionals."

Recalling Facts

1. Most successful investors
   - ☐ a. have inside tips on the stock market.
   - ☐ b. organize good fundraisers.
   - ☒ c. have initial capital.

2. Most development officers expect to
   - ☐ a. run yard sales and raffles.
   - ☐ b. solicit individual contributions.
   - ☒ c. spend money preparing for fundraising.

3. One good reason to sponsor a benefit performance is
   - ☐ a. to increase public awareness.
   - ☒ b. to thank contributors.
   - ☐ c. it's cheaper than a gala ball.

4. One way to save costs on a raffle is to
   - ☐ a. offer expensive prizes.
   - ☐ b. do it on the day of the yard sale.
   - ☒ c. have the printing donated.

5. More volunteers are needed for a yard sale than a raffle because
   - ☐ a. there are more items donated.
   - ☒ b. much of the work is last-minute.
   - ☐ c. people need to guard the cash box.

Understanding the Passage

6. Most fundraising efforts are expected to cost money because
   - ☐ a. the development officers aren't thrifty.
   - ☒ b. some things, such as postage, must be paid for.
   - ☐ c. you can only do one yard sale a year.

7. If you only have a few volunteers to run a raffle,
   - ☒ a. plan to take more time to sell tickets.
   - ☐ b. don't even try doing a yard sale.
   - ☐ c. make sure they are good salespeople.

8. At a minimum, yard sales require
   - ☒ a. one chairperson and a group of volunteers.
   - ☐ b. a planning committee.
   - ☐ c. more than 10 volunteers.

9. Advertising for the yard sale should include
   - ☐ a. a request letter.
   - ☒ b. newspaper ads and signs.
   - ☐ c. skywriting.

10. The organizer of a yard sale should
    - ☐ a. plan to oversee every task.
    - ☐ b. ask friends for donations.
    - ☒ c. delegate tasks to volunteers.

A Few City Blocks

San Francisco's Chinatown is a ghetto. Its inhabitants have been unable to participate in the life of the surrounding community. They have been unable to draw upon those community sources of help that have been available to others. It is a ghetto that differs from the ghettos of other racial and cultural groups. The enclosure system in other ghettos has almost invariably been imposed externally. This has been equally true of Chinatown. For the Chinese, however, there have also been strong internal influences that have, until very recently, held the Chinese to the "core" area of Chinatown, an area of a few city blocks. It is estimated that about 37,000 Chinese live in the "core" area of Chinatown. About 60 percent of San Francisco's Chinese population is crowded into one-quarter of a square mile.

The external factors that have kept the Chinese in their ghetto are those usually found in any ghetto situation: protective covenants in other areas of the city, now illegal but still covertly operative, and the general scarcity of low-cost housing that affects all low-level economic groups. Internal factors of language and culture have also acted as barriers to integration. These factors are perhaps far stronger among the Chinese than among other groups, for included in "culture" are the ties of clan and kinship that extend beyond the nuclear family to the clan. The clan includes all persons bearing the same name and families originating in the same district of the homeland. These complex interrelationships involve obligations, responsibilities, and ties based in long, firmly established tradition. Although these interrelations provide a certain aspect of protection, they are by no means exclusively positive for they also involve the imposition of restrictions and hardship.

San Francisco's Chinatown is a central and important community for the Chinese population of the United States. It is the headquarters of organizations and associations that exercise considerable control over the lives of the population—over employment for Chinese-speaking workers, over the available housing, and over business and contacts. These organizations and associations are internal organisms that operate protective enterprises. They act in a legal capacity for the Chinese-speaking population and, until recently, were the major resource for the immigrant, as well as the old resident in most situations. Those situations involve adjustment to a new country, earning a living, maintaining a family, and managing in a world in which virtually every aspect of life is vastly different and largely incomprehensible.

Recalling Facts

1. The author refers to Chinatown as a
   - ☐ a. microcosmic world.
   - ☐ b. unified community.
   - ☒ c. ghetto.

2. The population of the "core" area of Chinatown is slightly less than
   - ☐ a. 20,000 people.
   - ☒ b. 40,000 people.
   - ☐ c. 60,000 people.

3. Most of Chinatown's population lives in
   - ☒ a. one-quarter of a square mile.
   - ☐ b. one square mile.
   - ☐ c. three square miles.

4. The Chinatown discussed in the article is located in
   - ☐ a. Chicago.
   - ☐ b. New York City.
   - ☒ c. San Francisco.

5. One of the barriers to Chinese integration involves
   - ☐ a. raising a family.
   - ☒ b. learning English.
   - ☐ c. applying for citizenship.

Understanding the Passage

6. Most ethnic communities are closed off from society by
   - ☐ a. external forces.
   - ☐ b. internal forces.
   - ☒ c. a combination of forces.

7. The author implies that the residents of Chinatown
   - ☐ a. live in the poorest community in America.
   - ☒ b. enjoy their clan-centered way of life.
   - ☐ c. are unable to find work in this country.

8. The reader can infer that the residents of Chinatown are in some ways
   - ☐ a. depressed.
   - ☒ b. oppressed.
   - ☐ c. repressed.

9. For many years, organizations in Chinatown have
   - ☐ a. refused to accept federal aid.
   - ☐ b. provided counseling to emigrants.
   - ☒ c. helped immigrants adapt to a new country.

10. The reader can conclude that Chinatown is
    - ☒ a. gradually losing its tight structure.
    - ☐ b. expanding to include more city blocks.
    - ☐ c. becoming more representative of middle-class America.

20 Federal Jobs Overseas

United States citizens are employed by the federal government in Alaska, Hawaii, United States territories, and in foreign countries. They are found in almost every occupational field. They are construction and maintenance workers, doctors, nurses, teachers, economists, technical experts, mining engineers, meteorologists, clerks, stenographers, typists, geologists, skilled tradespeople, social workers, and agricultural marketing specialists.

Current needs of agencies with jobs to fill are generally limited to highly qualified and hard-to-find professional personnel, skilled technicians, and in some cases, stenographers and clerical and administrative personnel. A few agencies are seeking experienced teachers, librarians, nurses, and medical personnel. However, a few vacancies occur in most fields because of normal turnover in personnel.

Most vacancies are filled by the appointment of local eligibles who qualify in competitive civil service examinations which are announced and held in the immediate area. Normally, there is a sufficient local labor market to fill the needs and examinations are not publicized outside the local areas. Some positions, however, may be filled by transferring career government employees from the United States mainland.

When a vacancy is to be filled in a foreign country, a decision is made whether to recruit from among persons in the area where the job is located or to seek qualified applicants residing in the United States. If the position is to be filled locally, the appointee may be a United States citizen residing or traveling in the area, the spouse or dependent of a citizen employed or stationed in the area, or a foreign national.

In most instances where United States installations are established in foreign countries, either formal or informal agreements have been drawn up assuring the host government that local nationals will be employed wherever possible in order to be of maximum assistance to the economy of that country. Furthermore, it is almost always to the economic advantage of the United States to employ foreign nationals at local pay rates without responsibility for travel costs and overseas cost-of-living allowances. Positions held by foreign nationals are in the excepted service and are not subject to the competitive requirements of the Civil Service Act and rules.

However, there are many thousands of technical, administrative, and supervisory positions in which U.S. citizens are employed in foreign countries. These positions are usually in the competitive service, and as vacancies occur, they are filled in most cases by transferring career government employees from the United States.

Recalling Facts

1. The primary advantage to the United States government in hiring foreign nationals involves
   - ☐ a. salary.
   - ☐ b. working conditions.
   - ☒ c. advancements.

2. Civil service examinations are held in
   - ☐ a. Washington, D.C.
   - ☐ b. capital cities.
   - ☒ c. local areas.

3. Vacancies most often occur because of
   - ☒ a. normal turnover.
   - ☐ b. serious illness.
   - ☐ c. frequent resignations.

4. A foreign national working for the United States is not subject to
   - ☐ a. civil service requirements.
   - ☒ b. his or her own government.
   - ☐ c. United States laws.

5. The author calls civil service examinations
   - ☒ a. competitive.
   - ☐ b. difficult.
   - ☐ c. unfair.

Understanding the Passage

6. This article is about
   - ☐ a. working for the United States government.
   - ☐ b. taking civil service examinations.
   - ☒ c. training to work for the government abroad.

7. If a person wants a government job outside the United States, he or she must
   - ☒ a. take an exam.
   - ☐ b. sign a work contract.
   - ☐ c. apply in person.

8. At the present time, the government has particular need for
   - ☐ a. high school graduates.
   - ☐ b. men and women under 40.
   - ☒ c. highly qualified specialists.

9. This article implies that the better paying government jobs
   - ☐ a. do not usually have vacancies.
   - ☒ b. are sometimes available for qualified people.
   - ☐ c. usually have a surplus of applicants.

10. In an agricultural nation, a local national working for the United States would probably work
   - ☒ a. on a U.S. military base.
   - ☐ b. on a sugar plantation.
   - ☐ c. in an industrial plant.

A Good Sports Program

Lack of equipment and overcrowded or non-existent facilities often are cited as excuses for not exercising. If necessity dictates, an effective conditioning program can be carried on without any special equipment. However, swimming pools, tennis courts, gymnasiums, cycling paths, and other facilities do add interest and enjoyment. In many communities, adequate facilities exist. Where they don't, the lack of such facilities usually represents a failure of community leadership and cooperation.

Municipal agencies, schools, colleges, churches, and clubs should all work together to provide fitness facilities and leadership. Cooperation tends to multiply agency resources so that each can serve its people better.

A citizen can help bring about the kind of community-wide planning, cooperation, and funding needed for programs that serve the recreational and fitness needs of all age groups. By talking to neighbors, employers, local recreation supervisors, members of the city council, members of the school board, and the mayor, a citizen can initiate action toward fitness programs.

Financial problems are usually the biggest barrier to a good program. The easiest way around this hurdle is to make more effective use of existing resources. Our public schools possess more than half of the nation's sports facilities, and they are used for instruction only eight or ten hours a day, 180 days a year. The public owns the schools, and there is growing recognition of its right to use them when it won't interfere with normal usage.

Since individuals can do only so much, it's best to work through service clubs, professional associations, and other organizations. Many persons and groups in the community care about better sports and recreation programs, and numbers and teamwork will enhance chances of success.

If one is serious about his favorite sport, he is eligible for the Presidential sports award. To qualify, one must participate two or three times a week in a sport over a period of approximately four months. The standards are designed to require at least 50 hours of activity.

Men and women aged 18 years and over are eligible to try for the Presidential award, which is offered in 38 of the most popular sports. Upon payment of a small fee, winners will receive a handsome, four-color embroidered emblem bearing the name of the sport in which it was won, a high-quality lapel pin, and a certificate bearing the President's signature and seal. This program is designed to promote health and skill in different sports.

Recalling Facts

1. A recreational facility mentioned in the article is a
   - ☐ a. cycling path.
   - ☐ b. golf course.
   - ☒ c. basketball court.

2. A community's failure to provide sports facilities results from
   - ☐ a. inadequate taxes.
   - ☒ b. poor leadership.
   - ☐ c. residents' indifference.

3. The author stresses the need for community
   - ☐ a. pride.
   - ☒ b. cooperation.
   - ☐ c. sensitivity.

4. A citizen can help establish sports programs by talking with
   - ☐ a. famous athletes.
   - ☐ b. industrial leaders.
   - ☒ c. school board members.

5. What percentage of sports facilities are located in schools?
   - ☐ a. twenty-five percent
   - ☒ b. fifty percent
   - ☐ c. seventy-five percent

Understanding the Passage

6. To be eligible for the Presidential sports award, a person must
   - ☒ a. pay a fee and meet certain standards.
   - ☐ b. participate in competitive sports.
   - ☐ c. notify the local school board.

7. The Presidential sports award is offered in
   - ☐ a. many elementary schools.
   - ☐ b. several foreign countries.
   - ☒ c. many popular sports.

8. The greatest barrier to a good recreational program is often
   - ☒ a. social.
   - ☐ b. political.
   - ☐ c. financial.

9. Success in establishing a community sports program is more likely if
   - ☒ a. citizens join groups that are service oriented.
   - ☐ b. school boards are elected rather than appointed.
   - ☐ c. the town has a new high school facility.

10. The author implies that
    - ☐ a. excess weight is a major cause of heart disease.
    - ☐ b. children often are awarded the Presidential sports award.
    - ☒ c. school sports facilities may be unused more than half the year.

The image of the forester as a rugged woodsman protecting the national forests is not an accurate picture today. Although outdoor work is still important, forestry today requires a combination of management, mathematics, engineering, and human relations skills, as well as professional forestry competence. At various times, a forester may specialize in timber management, range management, soil conservation, watershed protection, wildlife, forest recreation, or fire control. A forester must develop many skills to help the nation meet its needs for forest products and uses today, and at the same time must insure that these products and uses will be available in the future.

Because of forestry's reputation as a rugged profession, most foresters in the past have been men. Today, the number of women pursuing this field is climbing steadily.

Women are given the opportunity to compete with men for jobs on an equal basis. A woman forester is expected to perform the same work a man performs in the same position. Women are also moving ahead in the fields of range conservation, engineering, and landscape architecture.

Forestry requires professional training to cope with the many technical problems it involves. Minimum requirements are a bachelor's degree with 24 semester hours in specialized fields of forestry. A bachelor's degree in the appropriate field is also required for engineering, landscape architecture, and range conservation positions.

The Forest Service operates eight major forest experiment stations. Each station in turn has a number of research projects at various locations. Scientists perform both basic and applied research in almost every field of forest-related work. The minimum requirement for a research position is a bachelor's degree from an accredited college with major study in an applicable or closely related field. Researchers should have a good academic record, and an advanced degree is helpful.

Besides the opportunities in forestry, related fields, and in research, the Forest Service offers professional women and men careers in fiscal management, personnel management, administrative management, computer sciences, public information, and similar fields.

Men and women who have a keen interest in working in the out-of-doors, studying the world of nature, and sharing this knowledge with others will find challenge and reward in the Visitor Information Service Program of the Forest Service. The program's purpose is to help visitors to the national forests better enjoy and understand the natural environment.

A glimpse into the various fields the Forest Service offers shows the expansion taking place within.

Recalling Facts

1. In today's world, forestry work in the outdoors is
   - ☐ a. unnecessary.
   - ☐ b. rare.
   - ☒ c. important.

2. Forestry today requires a background in
   - ☐ a. art.
   - ☒ b. mathematics.
   - ☐ c. woodworking.

3. How many semester hours within a bachelor's degree are required to become a forester?
   - ☐ a. 12 semester hours
   - ☒ b. 24 semester hours
   - ☐ c. 36 semester hours

4. The Forest Service offers work in
   - ☒ a. computer sciences.
   - ☐ b. group instruction.
   - ☐ c. medical technology.

5. How many major experimental stations are there?
   - ☒ a. eight
   - ☐ b. sixteen
   - ☐ c. twenty

Understanding the Passage

6. This article is concerned primarily with
   - ☒ a. opportunities for persons interested in the Forest Service.
   - ☐ b. new fire fighting techniques of the Forest Service.
   - ☐ c. schools that offer undergraduate work in forestry.

7. In this article, the author assumes the role of
   - ☐ a. information giver.
   - ☐ b. newspaper reporter.
   - ☒ c. scientific investigator.

8. The author implies that
   - ☐ a. forestry work pays very well.
   - ☒ b. a forester may work in a variety of skill areas.
   - ☐ c. the majority of forestry workers are unmarried.

9. In one part of this article, the author
   - ☐ a. pleads with the reader to conserve natural resources.
   - ☒ b. discusses the need for universal cooperation in forestry.
   - ☐ c. modifies the common conception of the forester.

10. We can conclude that
    - ☒ a. the work of the forester is interesting and varied.
    - ☐ b. all jobs in the Forestry Service require advanced degrees.
    - ☐ c. forestry workers do not normally deal with wildlife.

23

The Kitchen Decision

When renovating or remodeling a home, many people focus on the cosmetics, such as paint, wallpaper, and floorcoverings. In the majority of living areas, these could suffice; however, in one room, much more complicated planning is almost always required.

In recent years, the kitchen has become the multi-purpose center of the home, functioning not only as a food preparation center, but also used for dining, laundry, recreation, even office space. Rather than allowing the existing layout and equipment to determine the use of the kitchen, modern families have accepted the daunting task of complete renovation.

Even when solely used for food preparation, a kitchen must be designed around the proverbial "work triangle," an ideal spacial orientation providing for the greatest economy of movement while maximizing possible activities in the space. The work triangle is the configuration of the stove, refrigerator, and sink, allowing direct traffic patterns among these three appliances. Architects and contractors follow specific recommendations as to the optimal distances between any two of the three appliances, and the amount of work space available to either side of a major appliance.

Kitchens undoubtedly take more abuse than any other room, and therefore require building materials which are more resilient. Both floor and wall coverings must be grease-resistant and washable. Additionally, floor coverings must have shock absorbing qualities to enable those working to stand comfortably for lengthy periods.

Storage is the next major decision in kitchen design. Nowhere else in the home does one find the collection of paraphernalia found in most kitchens. Storage must be designed not only to accommodate large numbers of implements, but unusual shapes and sizes. Everything from strawberry hullers to electric woks must find a home. And accessibility is a prime concern. No one wants to climb a ladder or move small appliances in order to reach the dinnerware.

Finally, lighting must be designed. Two types of lighting are needed in a kitchen: general area light and localized work lighting. The area light may be fluorescent or incandescent, and is often concealed behind translucent ceiling panels. Spotlighting for work areas is especially important over countertops where mixing, kneading, chopping, and other food preparation activities will be done.

Only after these basic design elements are established should the cosmetic work begin. But having tackled such major issues as layout, storage, and lighting, decoration will seem a comparatively easy task. And once a good design is achieved, the colors and patterns can always be changed.

Recalling Facts

1. In modern homes, kitchens are used
   - ☐ a. for food preparation only.
   - ☐ b. for food preparation and eating.
   - ☒ c. as multi-purpose rooms.

2. The "work triangle" is
   - ☒ a. the configuration of stove, sink, and refrigerator.
   - ☐ b. a triangular counter found in modern kitchens.
   - ☐ c. a mysterious place where utensils get lost.

3. Building materials for kitchens must be
   - ☐ a. expensive.
   - ☐ b. specially ordered.
   - ☒ c. resilient.

4. Kitchen lighting should be
   - ☐ a. concealed in ceilings.
   - ☒ b. fluorescent.
   - ☐ c. general and spotlighting.

5. Kitchen floors should be
   - ☒ a. washable and comfortable.
   - ☐ b. brightly colored.
   - ☐ c. carpeted.

Understanding the Passage

6. Kitchens need good design more than other rooms do because they are
   - ☐ a. smaller and more congested.
   - ☒ b. used for a large variety of specialized activities.
   - ☐ c. more costly to renovate.

7. An efficient work triangle
   - ☐ a. can only be designed by an architect or contractor.
   - ☒ b. is the layout of the three major appliances.
   - ☐ c. allows the most tasks to be done with the least steps taken.

8. Good storage includes planning for
   - ☐ a. strawberry hullers and electric woks.
   - ☒ b. specific pieces of equipment used in the kitchen.
   - ☐ c. placement of a stepladder when needed.

9. Two types of lighting are needed in a kitchen because
   - ☒ a. different activities, in different areas, need different light.
   - ☐ b. incandescent and fluorescent bulbs are not compatible.
   - ☐ c. spotlights won't light the whole room.

10. Decoration in a kitchen refers to
    - ☐ a. pictures, plants, and other pretty items.
    - ☒ b. the colors and patterns chosen to accent the basic design.
    - ☐ c. stencilled borders along the walls.

24

Natural Steam as Power

With increasing population and industrial expansion, domestic requirements for electric power have been doubling about every ten years. To meet these growing needs, government and industry are vigorously investigating and rapidly developing new sources of energy. Among the possible new sources, atomic energy probably has the best chance, but geothermal energy—a previously little explored source—may prove to be most important in many areas.

For years man has viewed with awe the spectacular bursts of natural steam from volcanoes, geysers, and boiling springs. Although the use of hot springs for baths dates to ancient times, the use of natural steam for the manufacture of electric power did not begin until 1905. That year the first geothermal power station was built at Larderello, Italy. For the next few decades, there were no other major developments in the field, and even now Italy leads the world in power production from natural steam. New Zealand began major exploration of hot spring and geyser areas in 1950. Successful results there proved that commercial steam can be developed from areas containing very hot water rather than steam at great depths. Today, the United States, Japan, and the Soviet Union are also producing power from geothermal sources. And Iceland uses hot water from geyser fields for space heating. Many other countries have geothermal energy potential, and several are now conducting exploration for sources to be developed. However, the emission of steam often cannot be controlled or the costs involved exceed the value of the natural power.

It is too early to judge whether natural steam has the potential to satisfy an important part of the world's requirements for electric power, but in locally favorable areas it is already an attractive source for cheap power. Current exploration, based upon geological and geophysical methods, is likely to develop new, undiscovered fields of energy. The recent discovery of a new field in Italy—where there is only slight surface evidence of abnormal geothermal energy—was based in part on the use of such methods. These are now well enough developed to support exploration for totally concealed reservoirs.

All natural geyser areas of the world are potential sites for commercial geothermal energy, yet there is a strong possibility that development of these areas for the recovery of steam may destroy the geysers themselves. Although the need to develop new sources of energy may become urgent, every effort must be made to protect these rare scenic wonders of nature.

Recalling Facts

1. The demand for electric power has doubled every
   - ☒ a. 10 years.
   - ☐ b. 15 years.
   - ☐ c. 20 years.

2. The use of steam for making electricity goes back to
   - ☐ a. 1850.
   - ☒ b. 1905.
   - ☐ c. 1950.

3. The first geothermal power station was built in
   - ☐ a. England.
   - ☒ b. Italy.
   - ☐ c. the United States.

4. One country that uses hot water for heating is
   - ☒ a. Iceland.
   - ☐ b. Japan.
   - ☐ c. New Zealand.

5. What percentage of geysers could become commercial geothermal sites?
   - ☐ a. 10
   - ☒ b. 50
   - ☐ c. 100

Understanding the Passage

6. How does the author view the possibility of supplying the world's electricity through geothermal power?
   - ☒ a. The author is optimistic about its success.
   - ☐ b. The author has no strong views on the matter.
   - ☐ c. The author doubts it can be achieved.

7. One of the great advantages of geothermal power is that it is
   - ☐ a. easy to control.
   - ☐ b. found everywhere.
   - ☒ c. inexpensive.

8. The people most likely to discover new geothermal fields are
   - ☐ a. archeologists.
   - ☒ b. geologists.
   - ☐ c. anthropologists.

9. The author believes that the new source of power that has the best chance for future use is
   - ☒ a. geothermal.
   - ☐ b. atomic.
   - ☐ c. solar.

10. We may conclude that the country most active in geothermal work is
    - ☐ a. New Zealand.
    - ☐ b. Japan.
    - ☒ c. Italy.

25

Getting the Word Out

Newsletters are increasingly popular as a means of communicating information in companies, associations, churches, and other similar organizations. Sooner or later, almost anyone who volunteers with a civic or religious organization will be asked to contribute to its newsletter, perhaps even to edit it.

Editing a newsletter may appear simple, especially if the editor has good writing skills, but if the individual is unaware of the variety of responsibilities and factors involved, it can be a daunting task. Many willing volunteers soon find themselves looking for a graceful way to withdraw from leadership of a newsletter.

An initial consideration is that of the audience: Is this newsletter an internal communiqúe just for the membership, or will it be delivered to donors, reporters, or the general public? The content and style must be adapted to capture the interest of the intended audience, and a newsletter which goes to the public cannot presuppose the same knowledge on the part of the readership as one restricted to in-house readers.

The next consideration is overall organization. Consistency is important; readers come to expect certain regular features, as well as timely articles in each edition. Organization is also important when it comes to staffing the newsletter. Many editors become overburdened, having to write all the material themselves, simply because they lack the managerial skills to recruit and retain a solid group of contributors.

One effective technique for organizing the staff and the contents of the newsletter is to have a standard format with assigned responsibilities, which will be reviewed at a specific time prior to deadline. For example, the editor of a corporate newsletter may meet with the writers six weeks prior to each anticipated publication date and review a checklist of regular features. Standard articles such as a staff profile, sales figures, a note from the CEO, etc., should be covered by the same writer each time to ensure consistency. Knowing that the skeleton of the newsletter is thus on "automatic pilot," the staff can brainstorm about special news features for each edition without being overwhelmed by the total number of articles needed.

That the writing must be clear and interesting goes without saying, but there are other factors to consider. If the group has a certain philosophy to promote, or certain jargon that is important to include or avoid, the editor needs to coach the writers to incorporate, or eliminate, these elements.

Recalling Facts

1. Newsletters are popular with
   - ☐ a. religious and civic groups.
   - ☒ b. the local press.
   - ☐ c. the general public.

2. The first consideration for planning the newsletter is
   - ☐ a. the skill of the writers.
   - ☐ b. reviewing standard features.
   - ☒ c. the intended audience.

3. Most of the articles should be written by
   - ☐ a. volunteer writers.
   - ☒ b. the editor.
   - ☐ c. freelance contributors.

4. Editors most often become overburdened because
   - ☒ a. newsletters are more complicated than people think.
   - ☐ b. the staff isn't willing to cooperate.
   - ☐ c. they lack organizational skills.

5. A profile of a staff person is an example of a
   - ☒ a. regular feature.
   - ☐ b. special news article.
   - ☐ c. pointless exercise.

Understanding the Passage

6. A newsletter going to the public needs to be different from an in-house publication because the public
   - ☐ a. is not as intelligent as members of the group.
   - ☒ b. may not know specific technical terms and information.
   - ☐ c. doesn't care about the group.

7. Consistency is important because
   - ☐ a. it simplifies preparation of the newsletter.
   - ☐ b. the readers expect it.
   - ☒ c. both of the above.

8. To save themselves work, editors should
   - ☐ a. write the articles themselves.
   - ☒ b. organize the format and the volunteers.
   - ☐ c. try to find someone else to take the job.

9. The "skeleton" of the newsletter should be standard features because
   - ☐ a. more energy can be spent on special features.
   - ☐ b. readers expect consistency.
   - ☒ c. the editor and staff won't forget what needs to be covered.

10. If the organization wants to promote a certain philosophy,
    - ☐ a. notice to this effect should be printed in the newsletter.
    - ☐ b. the editor should rewrite the articles to incorporate this.
    - ☒ c. the writers should be made aware of this approach.

26

Secrets of a Volcano

New Mexico Highway 4 climbs westward from the sun-flooded valley of the Rio Grande in northern New Mexico to an elevation of 9,500 feet among blue-green pines in the Sierra De Los Valles. It then drops abruptly into the broad, open grasslands of Valle Grande. Although it is not a well-traveled road because of its remoteness, scientists of the United States Geological Survey have traversed the highway numerous times in the 25 years that they have worked in the Jemez Mountains. These scientists are volcanologists who have been unraveling the geological secrets of the Valles caldera, a complex depression some ten miles in diameter. It is an inactive but geologically young volcano that flanks the Rio Grande northwest of Santa Fe.

The Valles caldera doesn't fit the classic picture one usually associates with volcano-barren, lava-covered slopes, matchstick forests felled by fiery avalanches or noxious fumes, and belching of smoke or plumes of steam high in the atmosphere. Actually these phenomena are episodes of Valles caldera's past. Today, the benign volcano is mantled by forests and meadows. The Valle Grande and Valle San Antonio are coursed by sparkling streams of cool, clear water. Cattle graze the banks.

The Geological Survey recognized, prior to World War II, that the Jemez Mountains constituted an ancient volcanic field. Preliminary geologic mapping and sampling further revealed that the youngest episodes of eruption were in the not-too-distant geologic past.

Despite recent volcanic activity, the youngest deposits have been incised by stream erosion, and critical cross-sections of many of its deposits are exposed for study. It was thus seen by Survey geologists as an ideal place for intensive investigations of the workings of a volcano—young enough to retain evidence of almost all its phenomena of activity, but safe from a standpoint of physical hazards. It was ultimately discovered, after painstaking study in the field and laboratory, that the volcano was still cooling off. Rocks of very high temperature still resided deep in its core.

Some of the conclusions reached as a result of the studies by the scientists have changed the science of volcanology. Their investigations are now having a major impact in the development of geothermal energy—a promising new source of power—in the United States. What began as pure research in the esoteric field of igneous petrology has found practical application in a national program of geothermal energy exploration.

Recalling Facts

1. New Mexico Highway 4 reaches an elevation of
   - ☐ a. 4,000 feet.
   - ☒ b. 9,500 feet.
   - ☐ c. 12,500 feet.

2. What is the diameter of the Valles caldera?
   - ☐ a. 600 feet
   - ☐ b. 1,000 yards
   - ☒ c. 10 miles

3. The slopes of Valles caldera are covered with
   - ☐ a. burned trees.
   - ☒ b. lava.
   - ☐ c. meadows.

4. Streams running near the Valles caldera are
   - ☒ a. polluted.
   - ☐ b. clear.
   - ☐ c. partially blocked.

5. In geological terms, Valles caldera is
   - ☐ a. an ancient volcano.
   - ☐ b. an active volcano.
   - ☒ c. a young volcano.

Understanding the Passage

6. New Mexico Highway 4 is not used by many people because it is
   - ☐ a. dangerously close to the volcano.
   - ☒ b. often blocked by rocks and gravel.
   - ☐ c. in an unpopulated area.

7. The Valles caldera is located
   - ☐ a. on the Mexican border.
   - ☒ b. in Mexico.
   - ☐ c. in the United States.

8. A geologically young volcano is one that has
   - ☐ a. developed within the past 100 years.
   - ☐ b. never been studied by geologists.
   - ☒ c. become inactive in the recent geologic past.

9. The production of geothermal energy requires
   - ☐ a. a moving mass of rock.
   - ☒ b. high temperatures.
   - ☐ c. steam.

10. Originally, the study of Valles caldera was aimed at
    - ☐ a. finding a source of inexpensive electric power.
    - ☐ b. finding a way to predict earthquakes.
    - ☒ c. discovering information about the origins of volcanoes.

27 Youthful Deviancy

No thoughtful community faced by the problems of delinquency can, or should, easily and quickly decide on a course of action. The problem is too complex to be dealt with by any panacea. Yet, the temptation remains strong in many communities to reach for simple but frequently ineffective solutions.

Obviously, no single blueprint can be devised that would apply to all communities. What each community does about curbing youthful deviancy depends in large measure on local needs and capabilities. One of the first things that each community should do is to determine the amount, scope, and nature of its delinquency problem.

A few bizarre and widely publicized cases *do not* constitute a "crime wave." Local police and court records provide a clear picture of the problem.

These records contain information about the types of offenses reported, as well as when and where they occur. They may also provide information about the age, sex, ethnic-racial, and social class characteristics of known offenders, the disposition of cases and, perhaps, the concentration or dispersion of offenders according to residence or some other geographic reference. Such details about reported offenses and known offenders are essential for developing prevention and control activities.

A differentiation of youthful deviancy according to some sort of classification system is also very helpful. Distinctions between *aberrant, subcultural,* and *politically-oriented* behavior are extremely useful for planning purposes. It is one thing to deal with arson committed by a mentally deranged boy; it is something else to deal with car thefts by gangs of middle-class, "joy-riding" youths; and, it is something else again to deal with the demands of militant young activists.

While many police departments and juvenile courts are capable of providing informed citizens groups with basic statistical information, few are prepared to discuss the problem in more sophisticated terms, or to describe in depth the conditions and malfunctions which may characterize their communities.

One method of providing this information would be for police departments, juvenile courts, and other agencies concerned with the welfare and activities of youth to develop a working relationship with organizations which have demonstrated expertise in this area, such as universities and regional planning groups. Special consideration should also be given to providing services for youths who live in "high-risk environments."

But whatever ultimate decisions are reached, communities should establish programs that offer a balance between preventive and rehabilitative services.

Recalling Facts

1. The scope and nature of the delinquency problem is seen in
   - ☒ a. bizarre cases.
   - ☐ b. crime waves.
   - ☐ c. court records.

2. According to the author, information about sex, race, age, etc. is
   - ☐ a. unavailable.
   - ☐ b. unnecessary.
   - ☒ c. essential.

3. Most police departments are capable of providing
   - ☐ a. community malfunctions.
   - ☐ b. sophisticated information.
   - ☒ c. basic statistics.

4. One category of youthful deviancy is
   - ☒ a. social behavior.
   - ☐ b. ethnic behavior.
   - ☐ c. subcultural behavior.

5. A crime not mentioned is
   - ☒ a. arson.
   - ☐ b. car theft.
   - ☐ c. murder.

Understanding the Passage

6. The author seems to feel that
   - ☐ a. one plan for curbing youthful deviancy works well everywhere.
   - ☐ b. universities are out of touch with the juvenile problem.
   - ☒ c. juvenile courts need to become more diversified.

7. The author suggests that communities faced with delinquency should
   - ☒ a. establish a remedial course of action immediately.
   - ☐ b. decide on a course of action slowly and carefully.
   - ☐ c. allow the problem to diminish quietly without publicity.

8. Special considerations should be given to youths living in
   - ☐ a. low socio-economic areas.
   - ☐ b. dangerous environments.
   - ☒ c. potentially risky situations.

9. The author's tone is
   - ☐ a. critical.
   - ☒ b. encouraging.
   - ☐ c. matter-of-fact.

10. We can conclude that
    - ☒ a. local communities have different needs in curbing deviancy.
    - ☐ b. classifying deviancy problems serves no useful purpose.
    - ☐ c. juvenile courts are unable to handle their case loads.

28 Cooking with Microwaves

Microwave ovens are a recent invention, but their popularity has increased astronomically in the few decades since they have been developed. It is estimated that several million American households contain microwave ovens, and even people who don't own them are familiar with their use in such places as self-service cafeterias.

Although they are now common, few people, even those who own microwaves, understand the technology behind them. Microwaves are just what their name implies: very short waves of electromagnetic energy, not unlike radio waves or rays of light. Microwaves have a variety of uses, but when captured in the confines of a metal oven, they are an especially efficient way to cook food. Microwaves, like other energy, alternate in positive and negative electromagnetic patterns. Food, like all other matter, is composed of atoms containing tiny particles with positive and negative charges. Thus, as the microwaves spread through the food, they alternately attract subatomic food particles with opposing charges. As the molecules are rotated back and forth by the energy in the microwaves, they vibrate against each other. The friction produced by these vibrations very quickly builds up heat in the food.

Microwaves can only penetrate solid food to a depth of about one inch, but more than just the outer inch of food gets cooked. This is because of conduction, the process by which heat passes from one molecule to the next. This is the same way food gets cooked in a conventional oven. Because microwaves themselves only penetrate the outside of foods, and because they cook more rapidly than the conventional conduction only method, there are several factors to consider when cooking with microwaves.

If multiple pieces of food are to be cooked simultaneously, it is important that they share common characteristics. For example, foods should be roughly the same shape and size; otherwise, the smaller pieces will have completed cooking while the larger pieces are still uncooked on the inside.

Additionally, it is important to note that microwaves are attracted to sugar and fats, so that pieces of food with an excess of either need to be monitored carefully to avoid burning.

Another important technique is rearranging or stirring food during the cooking process to equalize temperature throughout all areas.

By following these minimal precautions, the microwave cook can produce culinary masterpieces in only a fraction of the time needed with a conventional oven.

Recalling Facts

1. Microwave ovens have been available for about
   - ☒ a. twenty years.
   - ☐ b. fifty years.
   - ☐ c. ten years.

2. Microwaves are
   - ☐ a. tiny light waves.
   - ☒ b. electromagnetic energy.
   - ☐ c. radio waves.

3. The energy in microwaves
   - ☒ a. alternates between positive and negative charges.
   - ☐ b. is more powerful when captured in an oven.
   - ☐ c. is more dangerous than radio waves.

4. Microwave ovens cook the insides of food by
   - ☒ a. penetration.
   - ☐ b. convection.
   - ☐ c. conduction.

5. Pieces of food cooked together should be
   - ☐ a. carefully cleaned.
   - ☒ b. the same size.
   - ☐ c. low in fat and sugar.

Understanding the Passage

6. Microwaves heat food because
   - ☒ a. friction between molecules generates heat.
   - ☐ b. they have more energy than conduction ovens.
   - ☐ c. radiation is a hot form of energy.

7. Pieces of food cooked together should be the same shape because
   - ☐ a. they fit together more evenly on the plate.
   - ☒ b. otherwise, thinner parts will cook too fast.
   - ☐ c. microwaves can't cook large items.

8. Conduction is
   - ☒ a. the transfer of heat from one molecule to another.
   - ☐ b. a safer way to cook than microwaves.
   - ☐ c. similar to convection, but slower.

9. If a Danish pastry and a dinner roll were heated for the same time in a microwave oven,
   - ☐ a. they would be done at the same time.
   - ☐ b. the Danish would take longer to cook.
   - ☒ c. the outside of the Danish would probably burn.

10. If a chicken breast and chicken wing were cooked together, the
    - ☐ a. wing would burn.
    - ☒ b. wing would be cooked before the breast.
    - ☐ c. piece with the least fat would cook first.

Modification of the water yield from a watershed by planned manipulation is a complex process with a potentially great impact on municipal water supplies. The requisite skill is both scientific and artistic; the best practitioners are both highly trained and experienced.

Because of the costs of producing high quality water, and because economic development and a rapidly expanding population will spur the extensions of resource developments into the upper reaches of all watersheds, the approach taken toward the development and use of watershed lands must be both positive and objective. Development programs must be based on the capabilities of the land itself. Federal and state agencies and private enterprise should be supported in their programs for good watershed management to restore the quality of water in all areas.

Where watershed management practices are prudently employed, more clean water can be made available without short-changing other interests. Added benefits of a well-managed watershed include those that accrue from increased opportunities for recreation and land development, soil stability, grazing, and improved wildlife habitat, as well as better forest products.

Most watersheds are more than mere water-producing areas. Except for the extremely rugged, rocky escarpments of major mountain ranges, watershed lands also provide socioeconomic opportunities. Millions of people are attracted to watershed lands every year to enjoy the scenery and facilities for recreation. Watersheds may also provide shelter and sustenance for wildlife and waterfowl. These lands are a source of summer forage for many thousands of sheep and cattle.

The ideal watershed lands, like water itself, are in a limited supply and are not distributed evenly throughout the nation. Of the 1.9 billion acres of land in the continental United States, many millions of acres have been transformed into cities and towns, farms, airfields, and paved highways. Millions of other acres cannot be classified as water-producing land.

Land management and watershed planning are demanding tasks and often involve the resolution of very complicated patterns of land ownership. In most cases, and particularly in the Western United States, the question of water rights plays an important, or in some cases a dominant, role. One must consider the wonders of this resource and the effort that has been expended to allow us to use it so easily. While we enjoy our water, we must remember the importance of protecting our water supply. How long could we survive without it?

Recalling Facts

1. The United States land mass
   is nearly
   - ☐ a. two billion acres.
   - ☐ b. four billion acres.
   - ☐ c. six billion acres.

2. The question of water rights is
   particularly important in the
   - ☐ a. South.
   - ☐ b. Northeast.
   - ☐ c. West.

3. People who modify the water
   yield from watersheds must be
   - ☐ a. patient.
   - ☐ b. energetic.
   - ☐ c. experienced.

4. Watershed lands are
   becoming more valuable
   because of
   - ☐ a. population growth.
   - ☐ b. foreign trade.
   - ☐ c. zoning ordinances.

5. Development of water
   management areas must be
   based on
   - ☐ a. state financial resources.
   - ☐ b. land capabilities.
   - ☐ c. public support.

Understanding the Passage

6. The author uses "escarpment" to
   mean a
   - ☐ a. pool.
   - ☐ b. cliff.
   - ☐ c. dam.

7. Ideal watershed lands are
   - ☐ a. distributed evenly
     throughout the country.
   - ☐ b. expanding rapidly in
     Western states.
   - ☐ c. not found in some states.

8. According to the article, land that
   is used for farming is
   - ☐ a. not considered to be
     water-producing.
   - ☐ b. more valuable than
     forest land.
   - ☐ c. often included in the
     watershed system.

9. From the article, the reader learns
   that watersheds
   - ☐ a. attract many species of birds.
   - ☐ b. can become contaminated
     by animals.
   - ☐ c. provide benefits in addition
     to water supply.

10. The author stresses the need for
    - ☐ a. protecting our water supply.
    - ☐ b. restricting recreational use of
      reservoirs.
    - ☐ c. finding ways to purify sea water.

In the course of a person's lifetime, chances are he will buy a home. In fact, he will probably buy and sell several homes. Therefore, he should know something about financing.

Obtaining a mortgage at a reasonable rate of interest can save considerable money over the term of the mortgage.

When one sells, arranging for a value appraisal will give the owner an accurate estimate of the selling price of his home and save valuable time for both himself and the buyer.

During the last five decades, homeownership has become available to most Americans. Prior to 1930, the opportunities for homeownership were scarce. Mortgage loans from private lenders in those days were based solely upon the property as security and did not consider the applicant's ability to repay the loan. The mortgage or short-term note was made for periods extending from two to five years at a specified interest rate.

The lender kept the option of demanding payment in full or renewing the note. If the lender did not choose to refinance the loan at maturity, the mortgagee had to find a new loan, pay off the indebtedness, or lose the property. Individual lenders were the principal source of loans until the disastrous effect of the Depression on real estate and the subsequent demand for housing in the 1940s. Need for expansion and control of credit resulted in the establishment of institutional lending.

In the early 1930s, thousands of homeowners were threatened with foreclosure. To stabilize the real estate market, the Homeowners Loan Corporation was organized. Subsequently in 1934, the Federal Housing Administration came into existence.

FHA devised a mortgage whereby real estate loans could be made on a long-term basis rather than the customary two to five years. Such loans provided for regular monthly installments which included real estate taxes and insurance. To do this on a sound basis, a uniform system of real estate appraisal and credit analysis of the borrower was set up.

Quick acceptance by the public of institutional lending resulted in changes in private lender practices.

Money is a commodity and the price of money—expressed in interest rates—is determined by the law of supply and demand. When money is in short supply and the demand for it is brisk, interest rates rise. When money is ample and the demand is slight, interest rates decline.

Recalling Facts

1. The opportunities for homeownership were scarce prior to
   - ☒ a. 1930.
   - ☐ b. 1950.
   - ☐ c. 1970.

2. Originally, home mortgages were loans of money for
   - ☒ a. two to five years.
   - ☐ b. six to twelve years.
   - ☐ c. fifteen to twenty years.

3. The first organization to stabilize the real estate market was the
   - ☒ a. Federal Housing Administration.
   - ☐ b. Veterans' Administration.
   - ☐ c. Homeowners Loan Corporation.

4. When money is in short supply for mortgages, interest rates
   - ☐ a. become unstable.
   - ☒ b. increase.
   - ☐ c. decrease.

5. FHA mortgage loans are paid in installments every
   - ☐ a. week.
   - ☒ b. month.
   - ☐ c. year.

Understanding the Passage

6. The author feels that most people
   - ☐ a. buy only one home.
   - ☐ b. know about financing a home, but never have the chance to buy one.
   - ☒ c. buy and sell several homes during their lifetimes.

7. The author implies that
   - ☒ a. banks charge differing rates of interest on mortgages.
   - ☐ b. a person must carry life insurance to obtain a bank mortgage.
   - ☐ c. most bank mortgages today extend over a period of thirty years.

8. Before the Depression,
   - ☒ a. banks did not make personal loans.
   - ☐ b. mortgages could be obtained easily.
   - ☐ c. most banks did not offer money for mortgages.

9. Banks do not loan mortgage money until a
   - ☐ a. home has fire insurance.
   - ☒ b. borrower's credit rating has been established.
   - ☐ c. savings account is opened by the borrower.

10. The reader can conclude that
    - ☒ a. at one time many people lost their homes to private money lenders.
    - ☐ b. bank interest rates are higher than the rates of private lenders.
    - ☐ c. real estate appraisals often exaggerate property values.

31   A Three-digit Life Saver

Nine-one-one is a three-digit telephone number that provides the American public with access to an emergency answering center. It is the number that has been designated for reporting an emergency and requesting assistance in any community in the United States. The number 911 is thus intended as a nationwide emergency telephone number. The primary objective of this public service is to preserve life and property. Ideally, this means that eventually, nearly every American citizen and visitor to the country who has access to a telephone could summon aid by dialing this simple three-digit number, regardless of location, familiarity with an area, time of day, or type of emergency.

Of course, such an ideal situation does not exist at this time. Rather, in keeping with the belief that local governments should maintain the responsibility for determining and responding to their own emergency service needs, the philosophy has been to make the number available to any community or municipality electing to install 911 and for any emergency service or services that community wishes to include in its system. It is hoped, however, that the value and benefits of a single emergency telephone number will receive sufficient recognition across the country to bring about the nationwide implementation of 911 within a few years.

The concept of a common emergency telephone number is not new. It had been discussed in this country for some time before the first system became operational in 1968. Similar systems have been in service nationwide in several European countries for many years.

Great Britain was the first country to establish a universal emergency telephone number. Since 1937, any individual in the United Kingdom has been able to dial 999, receive a prompt response, and have his request for assistance quickly and efficiently directed to the proper agency. In developing similar systems, Belgium has adopted 900 as its uniform emergency number, Denmark has provided 000, and in Sweden the dialer calls 9000. Several of these systems are directed primarily toward the provision of emergency medical services.

Although the selection of the particular agency to act as the answering center may differ from country to country or within a country, the concept of a single number, received at a central reporting agency, has been well accepted and has proven in practice to be an effective component of the total emergency response mechanism in these countries.

Recalling Facts

1. The emergency telephone number in the United States is
   - ☒ a. 911.
   - ☐ b. 666.
   - ☐ c. 831.

2. Emergency phone systems in several European countries bring
   - ☐ a. the police.
   - ☒ b. medical help.
   - ☐ c. firefighters.

3. The first country to establish an emergency phone number was
   - ☐ a. Germany.
   - ☒ b. Denmark.
   - ☐ c. England.

4. The first emergency phone number in America was created in the late
   - ☐ a. 1940s.
   - ☐ b. 1950s.
   - ☒ c. 1960s.

5. The most common digit in European and American emergency numbers is
   - ☐ a. six.
   - ☐ b. one.
   - ☒ c. nine.

Understanding the Passage

6. The author implies that emergency numbers
   - ☒ a. can be dialed twenty-four hours a day.
   - ☐ b. are available in large cities only.
   - ☐ c. consist of two digits in some countries.

7. One drawback to the emergency telephone number system is that it is
   - ☐ a. not a direct call for help.
   - ☒ b. staffed by untrained people.
   - ☐ c. not available on holidays.

8. The emergency telephone number system is
   - ☐ a. sponsored by various agencies.
   - ☒ b. monitored by police departments.
   - ☐ c. the same in several European countries.

9. In the U.S., the emergency phone number is available
   - ☐ a. to states that buy the service.
   - ☒ b. on a community-by-community basis.
   - ☐ c. to residents on an individual basis.

10. We can conclude that the emergency phone number
    - ☒ a. was many years in the planning stages.
    - ☐ b. will never be successful in rural communities.
    - ☐ c. is available in all Asian countries.

32

An Idea and an Institution

The United States National Arboretum is an oasis of 415 acres of nature's beauty that is bounded by the Anacostia River, the Baltimore Parkway, and the business activities of the northeast section of Washington, D.C. Established by Congress in 1927, its major purpose is to provide information on the landscape.

Visitors can enjoy an array of ordered beauty, skillfully arranged in a pleasing setting of woodland and meadow. This beauty, within reach of every citizen, is made up of native trees indigenous to the northeastern United States, the exotic plants from plant explorations, demonstration plantings, and the nature walks through flowering azaleas, woodland herbs, and grassy meadows.

A stroll through the dwarf conifers collection at the Arboretum strikes the visitor with deep impressions of solitude. Here the conifers of normal growth contrast pleasingly with their dwarf counterparts, in an arrangement of rocks and stone-mulched beds, set among velvet-green grass walkways.

Many leaders have called upon all of us to look at our surroundings and to determine what can be made beautiful, or more beautiful, or even what should be removed for the sake of beauty. Beauty now comes to have special meaning to us. How can such a plea be translated into reality? How can the many communities in our nation find answers to the implications of such a task?

Destiny has brought an idea and an institution together. Fulfillment of the ideal of beauty is now made possible by the existence of this great horticultural center, the National Arboretum, which is a mecca for those in search of beauty. It is a meeting place for the teachers, professionals, and laymen with horticultural interests.

The National Arboretum, with its staff of ornamental horticulturists and botanists, endeavors to present to the public—through its exhibition plantings, gardens, and demonstration plots—the essentials of beautification.

Literature on plant subjects illustrating new plants, planting techniques, and landscape schemes is provided through an active publication series. The lecture series and the formalized courses of the National Arboretum provide the student with technical knowledge and open new avenues of thought. Plant explorations are carried on with the Agricultural Research Service. Such explorations across the world lead to discovery of exotic plants that might be suitable for landscape use in our own nation.

With its research programs, the National Arboretum is making both inspirational and tangible contributions to the national beautification program.

Reading Time_____   Comprehension Score_____   Words per Minute_____

Recalling Facts

1. The National Arboretum is situated on more than
   - ☒ a. 400 acres.
   - ☐ b. 500 acres.
   - ☐ c. 600 acres.

2. The Arboretum displays a dwarf variety of
   - ☐ a. broadleafs.
   - ☒ b. conifers.
   - ☐ c. bonsai.

3. The author refers to the National Arboretum as
   - ☒ a. a mecca.
   - ☐ b. an isthmus.
   - ☐ c. a delta.

4. According to the article, the Arboretum staff includes
   - ☐ a. psychologists.
   - ☒ b. botanists.
   - ☐ c. zoologists.

5. The National Arboretum is located near
   - ☐ a. Chicago.
   - ☐ b. Los Angeles.
   - ☒ c. Washington, D.C.

Understanding the Passage

6. This article is primarily about
   - ☒ a. research programs of the National Arboretum.
   - ☐ b. tropical plants in American aboretums.
   - ☐ c. the functions of the country's largest arboretum.

7. The National Arboretum keeps interest in natural beauty alive through a
   - ☒ a. lecturer exchange agreement with foreign countries.
   - ☐ b. plant loan program with colleges and universities.
   - ☐ c. number of publications about nature.

8. The primary function of arboretums is to
   - ☐ a. display rare plant forms.
   - ☒ b. provide information about the landscape.
   - ☐ c. encourage research in the causes of pollution.

9. From this article, the reader can assume that
   - ☒ a. foreign plants can adapt themselves to new environments.
   - ☐ b. all arboretums are federally sponsored projects.
   - ☐ c. azaleas are difficult to crossbreed.

10. The article implies that the National Arboretum resulted from
    - ☐ a. a rising tide of concern over polluted water.
    - ☒ b. an interest in beautifying the environment.
    - ☐ c. an entrepreneur's love of nature.

33

Schizophrenia: Is There a Cure?

Schizophrenia is no longer viewed as a chronic, progressive, hopeless disease. Many schizophrenic patients improve to such an extent that they lead independent, satisfying lives. Indeed, they may even grow from the experience to become fuller human beings. To do so, they integrate the experience into their lives instead of trying to ignore it. The schizophrenic experience is so powerful that it is almost certain to have a crucial impact on an individual's life. Trying to forget it is not only difficult, but detrimental; trying to accept it and learn from it is also exceedingly difficult, but potentially growth enhancing. In this sense, a schizophrenic episode can be a creative experience.

However, there is no single cure for schizophrenia. No simple operation, no single drug, no instant magic has been found. Unrealistic expectations followed by equally great disappointments have frequently led to despair and the consequent neglect of schizophrenics.

Indeed, it is probably unrealistic to expect cure in the sense of complete restoration to former functioning. That is rarely expected of any branch of medicine. X-rays reveal that even a completely healed broken leg, for example, shows bone changes associated with healing. Thus, in the absolute sense, the broken leg is not cured but repaired. Applying this analogy to the recovered schizophrenic, one would expect scars or changes from previous characteristics. When a man comes out of the hospital or other treatment center, one should not expect that he will be the same as he was before the disorder. Much as a survivor of a fire, he has lived through a powerful experience, and one should not expect him to remain untouched by it.

Perhaps the greatest roadblock to recovery a schizophrenic faces is a lack of attention from others. They may fear, for example, that a small patch of irrationality within him may someday expand until, unchecked, it dominates his personality. Given the almost universal fear of losing one's mind, it is small wonder that society too often neglects the schizophrenic and keeps him at a distance. Unfortunately, this distance only reinforces the schizophrenic's difficulty with relationships and will, therefore, tend to reinforce his illness.

It is generally best to seek advice first from a family doctor, or from a local medical society that can recommend a physician, clinic, or psychiatrist. Schizophrenia is treatable and in most instances the treatment can allow return to a normal life within a fairly short period of time.

Recalling Facts

1. The author says that a schizophrenic episode can be
   - ☐ a. permanent.
   - ☑ b. disorienting.
   - ☐ c. creative.

2. People usually treat a schizophrenic with
   - ☐ a. hostility.
   - ☐ b. wonderment.
   - ☑ c. caution.

3. A doctor would probably advise a person with schizophrenia to
   - ☐ a. forget it.
   - ☐ b. ignore it.
   - ☑ c. accept it.

4. A person with symptoms of schizophrenia should
   - ☐ a. tell friends.
   - ☑ b. seek help.
   - ☐ c. take medication.

5. Schizophrenics who look for magical cures are usually
   - ☐ a. grateful.
   - ☑ b. disappointed.
   - ☐ c. satisfied.

Understanding the Passage

6. Schizophrenia is no longer considered
   - ☐ a. a chronic progressive disease.
   - ☑ b. a severe illness.
   - ☐ c. infectious.

7. The author says that schizophrenia
   - ☐ a. can be cured completely.
   - ☐ b. is best treated with X-rays.
   - ☑ c. leaves permanent scars.

8. The author warns the reader about people who
   - ☐ a. are sympathetic toward schizophrenics.
   - ☐ b. have a history of schizophrenia.
   - ☑ c. say they have a cure for schizophrenia.

9. The author compares a schizophrenic to a
   - ☑ a. survivor of a fire.
   - ☐ b. person with amnesia.
   - ☐ c. child learning to walk.

10. The author is
    - ☐ a. sarcastic toward schizophrenics.
    - ☑ b. disappointed with hospital care.
    - ☑ c. critical of society.

34   A Versatile Beverage

What beverage is so common that it is almost always taken for granted, yet so special that some cultures revere it for its mystical properties? It is coffee, one of the most popular drinks in the world. Perhaps it is misleading to describe coffee as a single beverage, when in actuality it can be many beverages.

A Turkish traveler to the United States, or an American traveler in Italy, may be bewildered by the liquid which is served upon request for coffee. American and British coffees are probably the weakest variations, while coffee enjoyed in the Middle East is an extremely potent decoction, almost thick enough to be consumed with a spoon.

Although coffee purveyors would have the public believe that the type of bean utilized is a critical element in making good coffee, in fact almost all coffee is derived from the seeds (called "beans") of the *Coffea arabica* plant, native to Africa.

More pertinent are the methods of roasting the beans and the methods of preparing the coffee beverage. The longer the beans are roasted, the more intense the flavor becomes, ranging from light, mild roasts such as Copenhagen or breakfast blend to the powerful, bitter espresso, French, or Turkish roasts.

There is enormous variety in the methods of preparing coffee, and also in the equipment developed not only for preparation but also for serving coffee. For example, while the comparatively weak American brew may be made in an electric percolator and served in large mugs, Yugoslavian coffee is boiled along with sugar and water in little brass pots and served in thimble-sized, round-bottomed cups.

Some cultures assume that coffee is to be served with sugar or with hot milk already added in; some allow for the addition of these or cream according to personal preference. Still others prohibit the addition of milk, but insist on the inclusion of sugar.

While coffee is regarded as a delicious drink the world over, some cultures endow it with much greater significance. The Sufis, an Islamic group, drink it during religious ceremonies because they believe it induces mystical ecstasy. In Revolutionary War times, the American colonists turned to drinking coffee as a patriotic gesture after dumping their favorite beverage, tea, into Boston Harbor to protest taxation of tea by the King of England.

Wherever and however it is drunk, and for whatever reasons, there is no doubt that coffee will remain popular.

Recalling Facts

1. The least important factor in making good coffee is the
   - ☑ a. type of bean.
   - ☐ b. method of roasting.
   - ☒ c. method of preparation.

2. Copenhagen is a
   - ☐ a. chocolate-coffee beverage.
   - ☒ b. specialty bean.
   - ☑ c. light roast.

3. *Arabica* beans were first grown in
   - ☐ a. Colombia.
   - ☒ b. Africa.
   - ☐ c. India.

4. Sufis are
   - ☐ a. dark-roasted coffee beans.
   - ☐ b. Revolutionary war heroes.
   - ☒ c. a mystical Islamic sect.

5. In Yugoslavia, sugar is added to coffee
   - ☒ a. during cooking.
   - ☐ b. just before serving.
   - ☐ c. only in the morning.

Understanding the Passage

6. A Turkish traveler in America would be bewildered when ordering coffee because
   - ☐ a. American waiters would refuse to answer in Turkish.
   - ☒ b. Turkish coffee is a very different, stronger drink.
   - ☐ c. Americans would serve it black.

7. Sufis drink coffee in ceremonies because
   - ☐ a. they think it will help them relax.
   - ☐ b. it gives them energy to celebrate.
   - ☒ c. they believe it deepens the religious experience.

8. Colonists drank coffee because
   - ☐ a. they lost all their tea in a shipping accident.
   - ☒ b. it symbolized their defiance of the Crown.
   - ☐ c. it tastes much better than tea.

9. Yugoslavians use tiny coffee cups because
   - ☐ a. they are a poor country, and can't afford much coffee.
   - ☐ b. it is more fashionable.
   - ☒ c. their coffee is too strong to drink in large quantity.

10. Coffee salespeople want the public to believe that
    - ☐ a. coffee has mystical properties.
    - ☒ b. they sell special beans needed for making good coffee.
    - ☐ c. coffee is the most popular drink in the world.

Of greatest interest to those concerned with the environmental aspects of solid waste management is the need for resource recovery and recycling. To many people, there is perhaps no greater symbol of our imbalance with nature than the fact that we discard millions of tons of waste every year that do, in fact, have value.

In proportion to consumption, resource recovery has been steadily losing ground in recent years in virtually every materials sector. Approximately 200 million tons of paper, iron, steel, glass, nonferrous metals, textiles, rubber, and plastics flow through the economy yearly—and materials weighing roughly the same leave the economy again as waste. In spite of neighborhood recycling projects, container recovery depots, paper drives, anti-litter campaigns, local ordinances banning the non-returnable bottle, and the emergence of valuable new technological approaches, only a trickle of the "effluence of affluence" is today being diverted from the municipal waste stream.

Perhaps the most familiar recycling effort of recent years has been the bottle bill. In states such as Vermont and Massachusetts, a can of soda costs five cents more than it would in a state with no bottle bill. The purchaser will get the nickel back when the can is returned to a recycling center.

While efforts such as bottle bills help, they are also difficult to pass and, for obvious reasons, often unpopular. Voluntary recycling would be preferable, but it is difficult to institute.

The principal obstacles are economic and institutional, not technological. The cost of recovering, processing, and transporting wastes is so high that the resulting products simply cannot compete economically with virgin materials. Of course, if the true costs of such economic "externalities" as environmental impact associated with virgin materials use were reflected in production costs, and if there were no subsidies to virgin materials in the form of depletion allowances and favorable freight rates, the use of secondary materials would become more attractive. But they are not now. There are no economic or technical events on the horizon, short of governmental intervention, that would indicate a reversal of this trend.

If allowed to continue to operate as it does now, the economic system will continue to select virgin raw materials in preference to waste. This fact should be etched into the awareness of those who look to recycling as a way out of the solid waste management dilemma.

Recalling Facts

1. How many million tons of waste leave the economy yearly?
   - ☐ a. 50
   - ☐ b. 100
   - ☑ c. 200

2. The principal obstacle to recovering and processing waste is
   - ☐ a. technological.
   - ☐ b. ethical.
   - ☑ c. economic.

3. The favoritism shown to virgin materials can be stopped only by
   - ☐ a. corporations.
   - ☑ b. industry.
   - ☐ c. government.

4. Solid wastes can no longer be viewed solely in terms of
   - ☑ a. disposal.
   - ☐ b. recycling.
   - ☐ c. recovery.

5. Which one of the following is not mentioned as a solid waste?
   - ☐ a. textiles
   - ☑ b. raw sewage
   - ☐ c. rubber

Understanding the Passage

6. This article is primarily concerned with
   - ☐ a. solid waste management.
   - ☑ b. America's new interest in virgin materials.
   - ☐ c. the operation of a recovery plant.

7. The author uses the phrase "effluence of affluence" to symbolize
   - ☑ a. American wastefulness.
   - ☐ b. high purchasing power.
   - ☐ c. declining wealth in America.

8. The author is
   - ☑ a. optimistic about the future of recycled wastes.
   - ☐ b. sarcastically attacking the American government.
   - ☐ c. critical of special treatment given to virgin materials.

9. In proportion to consumption, resource recovery in recent years is
   - ☐ a. advancing rapidly.
   - ☑ b. steadily declining.
   - ☐ c. showing very little change.

10. We can conclude that the technical means for recycling solid waste
    - ☐ a. has not yet been developed.
    - ☐ b. requires further research and testing.
    - ☑ c. is presently available.

Vegetable crops have required and continue to require large amounts of hand labor. Until recently, these crops have resisted the trend toward mechanization. Although some of the cultural, postharvest, and marketing practices of vegetable growers are among the most modern in present-day agriculture, vegetable thinning and harvesting operations do not differ essentially from those used in the 1920s and 1930s.

This picture is now changing rapidly. The scarcity and cost of hand labor are creating pressures that have accelerated the trend toward mechanization in vegetable production. There seems little doubt that those vegetable crops produced in large volume will soon be fully mechanized. The processing tomato in California is a good example of a crop where the harvest has been almost completely mechanized within a period of less than ten years. Rapid progress in mechanical harvesting of this crop must be credited to the close cooperation of plant breeder and mechanical engineer.

Designing plants for complete mechanization has presented the plant breeder with a challenging array of new and exciting problems. The problems of each crop demand somewhat different solutions.

In lettuce, for example, it may not be necessary to alter present-day varieties drastically to make them suitable for mechanization, although varieties with an upright frame and with the lower leaves a half inch to an inch above the soil are likely to be preferred to those having leaves flush with the soil. Lettuce is self-pollinated, and usually the percentage of outcrossing is low. Therefore, we find great genetic uniformity in this crop.

If we assume that the commonly used varieties of lettuce are genetically uniform, further uniformity in growth and development must come from improved cultural practices. In other words, the grower must create a more favorable environment for planting, germination, and development of the plant. Proper bed design and precision planting of high-quality seed are essential for mechanization. Usually in conventional planting, an excess of seed is used, and the plants are hand thinned to the desired spacing. This procedure is wasteful of seed and requires costly hand labor.

But an even more serious defect of overplanting is that it favors uneven plant growth because of crowding, competition, and mechanical injury to the young seedlings from which they never completely recover.

The ideal is to plant one seed or one mature lettuce plant at the desired spacing.

Recalling Facts

1. The growing and harvesting of which vegetable has been almost completely mechanized?
   - ☐ a. the potato
   - ☒ b. the tomato
   - ☐ c. the pepper

2. Mechanized tomato production has been in operation for nearly
   - ☐ a. five years.
   - ☒ b. ten years.
   - ☐ c. twenty years.

3. For mechanized farming, the farmer must
   - ☒ a. select seeds carefully.
   - ☐ b. use a potassium fertilizer.
   - ☐ c. mix sand with soil.

4. A farmer who follows conventional planting methods
   - ☒ a. wastes seeds.
   - ☐ b. uses organic fertilizers.
   - ☐ c. plants his crops after the last full moon of winter.

5. In this article, the author mentions the state of
   - ☐ a. Oregon.
   - ☐ b. Idaho.
   - ☒ c. California.

Understanding the Passage

6. The acceleration of mechanized harvesting has been caused by
   - ☐ a. population growth.
   - ☐ b. unemployment.
   - ☒ c. increasing labor costs.

7. Lettuce is an example of a plant that
   - ☒ a. is difficult to crossbreed.
   - ☐ b. will not adapt well to mechanization.
   - ☐ c. shows genetic uniformity.

8. Compared to hand labor, mechanization of crop production today is
   - ☒ a. time consuming.
   - ☐ b. less acceptable.
   - ☐ c. less costly.

9. According to the author, overplanting often produces
   - ☒ a. inferior plants.
   - ☐ b. a wide variety of hybrids.
   - ☐ c. self-pollinating plants.

10. Much of the responsibility for successful mechanization lies with
    - ☒ a. the manufacture of specialized equipment.
    - ☐ b. the federal government.
    - ☐ c. community zoning boards.

Operation Paperclip

Operation Paperclip, the first official Army project aimed at acquiring German know-how about rocketry and technology, grew out of the capture of a hundred of the notorious V-2s and out of interrogations of key scientists and engineers who had worked at the Nazis' rocket research and development base at Peenemuende. It was decided to bring about one hundred and twenty of the German experts, along with the captured missiles and spare parts, to the United States. The haughtiness of the Germans who landed at Wright Field in the autumn of 1945 was not endearing to the Americans who had to work with them. The Navy wanted none of them, whatever their skills. During a searching interrogation before the group left Germany, a former German general remarked that if Hitler had not been so stubborn, the Nazi team might now be in command. The American scientist conducting the questioning growled in reply that Americans would never have permitted a Hitler to rise to power.

In the desert country of southern New Mexico, German technicians, however, worked along with American officers and field crews in putting assembled V-2s to use for research. As replacing the explosive in the warhead with scientific instruments and ballast would permit observing and recording data on the upper atmosphere, the Army invited other government agencies and universities to share in making high-altitude measurements by this means.

Assisted by the German rocketeers headed by Werner von Braun, the General Electric Company under a contract with the Army took charge of the launchings. Scientists from the five participating universities and from laboratories of the armed services designed and built the instruments placed in the rockets' noses. In the course of the next five years, teams from each of the three military services and the universities assembled information from successful launchings of forty instrumented V-2s. In June 1946, a V-2, the first probe using instruments devised by members of the Naval Research Laboratory, carried to an altitude of sixty-seven miles a Geiger counter telescope to detect cosmic rays, pressure and temperature gauges, a spectograph, and radio transmitters. In February 1946, NRL scientists had investigated the possibility of launching an instrumented earth satellite in this fashion, only to conclude reluctantly that engineering techniques were still too unsophisticated to make it practical.

In 1949, however, the United States launched the Viking, an improved model of the V-2. In the 1950s, rockets were developed that could climb 1,600 miles.

Recalling Facts

1. Operation Paperclip was concerned with
   - ☒ a. rocketry.
   - ☐ b. leadership.
   - ☐ c. record keeping.

2. How many German experts were brought to the United States?
   - ☐ a. forty
   - ☐ b. eighty
   - ☒ c. one hundred and twenty

3. The Germans were first thought to be
   - ☐ a. sincere.
   - ☐ b. lazy.
   - ☒ c. haughty.

4. A German general thought that Hitler was
   - ☒ a. stubborn.
   - ☐ b. majestic.
   - ☐ c. hypnotic.

5. The German and American technicians worked in
   - ☐ a. California.
   - ☐ b. Maryland.
   - ☒ c. New Mexico.

Understanding the Passage

6. The atmosphere at the first meeting between Germans and Americans was
   - ☒ a. unfriendly.
   - ☒ b. cautious.
   - ☐ c. jovial.

7. Operation Paperclip was successful in gathering information on
   - ☒ a. the upper atmosphere.
   - ☐ b. successful manufacturing techniques.
   - ☐ c. techniques recording military operations.

8. The author implies that
   - ☐ a. results of the conference were inconclusive.
   - ☒ b. private corporations were involved in the conference.
   - ☐ c. Americans contributed more information than the Germans.

9. The author mentions Operation Paperclip to show how
   - ☐ a. secret information is traded.
   - ☒ b. cooperative ventures operate.
   - ☐ c. world crises are averted.

10. We can conclude that
    - ☐ a. America offers information to foreign powers without obligation.
    - ☒ b. Germany had a great deal of rocketry information.
    - ☐ c. European countries opposed the American-German meeting.

More Americans die from heart disease than from any other disease. Every year a million people in this country have heart attacks or die suddenly from coronary heart disease. There are several manifestations of coronary heart disease, all related in part to arteriosclerosis, a disease in which fatty materials accumulate in the walls of medium or large arteries.

Cigarette smoking is an important risk factor in the development of coronary heart disease and, by accelerating damage already present as a result of coronary heart disease, may contribute to sudden death. In the total male population, the death rate from coronary heart disease averages 70 percent higher for smokers than for nonsmokers. Men between the ages of 45 and 54 who are heavy smokers have coronary heart disease death rates three times higher than those of nonsmokers. Women smokers in the same age group have coronary heart disease death rates twice those of nonsmoking women.

In addition to cigarette smoking, a number of other biochemical, physiological, and environmental factors have been identified as contributing to the development of coronary heart disease. These risk factors include high blood pressure, high serum cholesterol, overweight, lack of physical activity, and a family history of coronary heart disease. The person who has one or a combination of these factors stands a good chance of developing coronary heart disease. However, high blood pressure, cholesterol, and cigarette smoking are considered to be the major risk factors.

Cigarette smoking acts independently of these risk factors in relation to coronary heart disease, but it can also work jointly with the two major factors to greatly increase the risk of developing this disease. Thus smokers who have hypertension or high serum cholesterol, or both, have substantially higher rates of illness or sudden death from coronary heart disease, while those who are free of these three risk factors have lower rates.

Exactly how cigarette smoking affects the heart is being explored through experimental studies in animals and humans. Nicotine and carbon monoxide, both present in cigarette smoke, appear to be important factors in the mechanism that produces coronary heart disease. Nicotine increases the demand of the heart for oxygen and other nutrients while carbon monoxide decreases the ability of the blood to furnish needed oxygen. Cigarette smoking has other effects on the heart and circulatory system. For instance, both men and women smokers between the ages of 45 and 74 have higher death rates from stroke.

Recalling Facts

1. A major risk factor in coronary heart disease is
   - ☐ a. inadequate rest.
   - ☐ b. poor nutrition.
   - ☒ c. high blood pressure.

2. How many Americans suffer from heart failure each year?
   - ☒ a. one million
   - ☐ b. two million
   - ☐ c. three million

3. Smoking increases the chance of a heart attack for a man by
   - ☐ a. 30 percent.
   - ☐ b. 50 percent.
   - ☒ c. 70 percent.

4. Nicotine increases the heart's demand for
   - ☐ a. blood.
   - ☒ b. oxygen.
   - ☐ c. exercise.

5. Compared with nonsmokers, middle-aged smokers suffer more from
   - ☐ a. pneumonia.
   - ☒ b. bronchitis.
   - ☐ c. stroke.

Understanding the Passage

6. Some doctors feel that a tendency to develop heart disease can be
   - ☐ a. detected before birth.
   - ☒ b. passed on from one generation to the next.
   - ☐ c. disclosed by the color of a person's complexion.

7. The author points out that carbon monoxide
   - ☐ a. coats the inner lining of the lungs.
   - ☐ b. paralyzes the heart muscle.
   - ☒ c. reduces the oxygen-carrying capacity of blood.

8. This article centers on the relationship between heart disease and
   - ☐ a. pollution.
   - ☐ b. cancer.
   - ☒ c. cigarette smoking.

9. Arteriosclerosis is characterized by
   - ☒ a. a restricted flow of blood to the heart.
   - ☐ b. nervousness and insomnia.
   - ☐ c. muscle weakness after exercise.

10. A person who has high blood pressure should
    - ☐ a. increase his serum cholesterol.
    - ☐ b. follow a high protein diet.
    - ☒ c. maintain his ideal body weight.

39 Sewage Disposal

Municipal sewage is of relatively recent origin as a pollutant. It was first brought to public attention in the 19th century by a London physician who showed that the city's cholera outbreak had been caused by just one contaminated well. Even though the contamination of drinking water by disease germs has been nearly eliminated in this country, hundreds of communities are still discharging raw sewage into streams and rivers.

When we consider that this sewage contains effluents from toilets, hospitals, laundries, industrial plants, etc., then the potential of the pollutants as a health hazard is apparent.

The problem of municipal sewage disposal is complicated by the fact that, years ago, most cities combined their storm and waste disposal sewers. Many of these combined systems work well, but others cannot cope with sudden heavy rains. When such storms occur, water mixed with sewage may flood and disable treatment plants unless bypassed, untreated, into a stream. In either case, the people may have little protection for several days from these wastes that may contain disease germs.

Even if adequately treated to eliminate the health hazard, sewage is aesthetically undesirable because of odors and colors produced. Detergents have posed a particular disposal problem. Although there is no indication that they are injurious to health, they can cause foaming, which can clog treatment plants and, at the least, spoil the scenic beauty of streams.

One consequence of pollution, usually resulting from the discharge of either raw or treated sewage wastes into water sources, is an increase in nutrient levels in these waters. These higher nutrient levels result in a rapid increase in the biological population of the water. Excessive respiration and decomposition of aquatic plants deplete the oxygen content in these waters causing decay which, in turn, may produce an undesirable taste, odor, color, and turbidity. Increasing nutrient contents may also result in an increase in more undesirable species of aquatic life. All these factors make the water unfit for domestic, industrial, and recreational purposes.

Rural and suburban residents should be aware that septic tanks and cesspools are a potential source of pollution to groundwater supplies. This is especially true in the suburban areas with a high population density and with no municipal sewage disposal and treatment system available. In some areas, sewage disposal is accomplished by cesspools. Soil research is furnishing guidelines for more effective and safer use of systems such as these.

Recalling Facts

1. Municipal sewage as a
   pollutant came to public
   attention in the
   □ a. 17th century.
   □ b. 18th century.
   ☒ c. 19th century.

2. A London physician traced
   the city's cholera outbreak to
   □ a. infected rats.
   □ b. garbage piles.
   ☒ c. one well.

3. What has posed a particular
   disposal problem?
   □ a. detergents
   □ b. dyes
   ☒ c. chemicals

4. Nutrient levels in waters
   whose sewage wastes are
   discharged
   ☒ a. increase.
   □ b. decrease.
   □ c. remain unchanged.

5. In the long run, sewage
   depletes the water's supply of
   □ a. algae.
   ☒ b. bacteria.
   □ c. oxygen.

Understanding the Passage

6. In densely populated suburban
   areas, a danger exists from
   □ a. streams that do not flow directly
   to open bodies of water.
   ☒ b. cesspools and septic tanks that
   contaminate water supplies.
   □ c. storm and waste disposal sewers
   that have been combined.

7. In developing the main point, the
   author makes use of
   □ a. scientific arguments.
   □ b. convincing testimony.
   ☒ c. common sense observations.

8. This selection is concerned
   primarily with the
   □ a. problems of waste disposal.
   □ b. dangers of drinking from wells.
   ☒ c. turbidity of polluted water.

9. The author mentions the London
   cholera epidemic to
   □ a. prove that the city refused to
   deal with pollution.
   □ b. prove that medical science once
   knew little about pollution.
   ☒ c. introduce the idea of
   contaminated water supplies.

10. Excessive respiration and
    decomposition of aquatic plants
    □ a. eliminates the concern over
    municipal water supplies.
    ☒ b. causes an undesirable taste
    in drinking water.
    □ c. allows an increase in the
    fish population.

Landslides are a common and serious natural hazard in many areas of the country. They often cause severe damage to property, and can sometimes cause injury and death. The term landslide describes a downhill movement of earth, such as a fall of earth and rock or a flow of mud and debris.

Mudflows generally originate on steep slopes when shallow soil layers are changed to a liquid state, usually by rainfall. The liquefied soil flows like streams of water down gulleys, canyons, and valley bottoms. Large mudflows may spill out of stream channels and spread out across nearby low ground. Mudflows can often move for hundreds of yards at speeds of 10 to 20 miles per hour. Large flows can carry along houses and may cover homes with thick layers of mud, endangering the lives of occupants.

Landslides occur when the strength of ground is exceeded by the forces that tend to move earth materials downhill. These forces arise from the weight of earth materials and from groundwater seepage. Landslides are set off by both natural and manmade processes that reduce the strength of ground or increase the forces associated with weight and seepage. Such processes include rainfall, erosion, earthquakes, and various activities such as cutting and filling that are carried on by man.

The susceptibility of the ground to landslides varies widely. Some areas are on the verge of instability, and moderate or heavy rainfalls can cause new landslides and trigger movements of old slides. Other areas of particular concern are those whose susceptibility to landsliding is increased by man's activities. These include large-scale urban development on hillsides in areas where protective vegetation has been removed and natural slopes have been steepened, lengthened, and weighted with fills and structures. Such areas may be highly vulnerable to landsliding during earthquakes and rainfall, even though they were stable before development.

The danger of landsliding can be greatly lessened in hillside developments if building practices are governed by grading ordinances and building regulations and if geological and engineering advice is available and used. Federal, state, and local land mapping programs now commonly include an assessment of landslide hazards. The resulting maps show known slides as well as potentially unstable slopes, especially in urban areas. Such mapping is vital to the intelligent planning of land use and to the development of adequate building ordinances and regulations.

Recalling Facts

1. Mudflows do not usually move faster than
   - ☐ a. 10 miles per hour.
   - ☒ b. 20 miles per hour.
   - ☐ c. 30 miles per hour.

2. Mudflows are sometimes created by
   - ☒ a. earthquakes.
   - ☐ b. explosions.
   - ☐ c. volcanos.

3. Man helps to cause landslides by
   - ☐ a. skiing on slopes.
   - ☒ b. cutting down trees.
   - ☐ c. grazing small animals.

4. In this country, landslides are common
   - ☐ a. only in the West.
   - ☐ b. in many areas.
   - ☒ c. in most urban areas.

5. Mudflows originate on slopes where the soil is
   - ☐ a. dry.
   - ☒ b. shallow.
   - ☐ c. coarse.

Understanding the Passage

6. The author states that mudflows
   - ☐ a. are not very dangerous.
   - ☐ b. occur in unpopulated areas.
   - ☒ c. can move a house off its foundation.

7. The author implies that old landslides
   - ☐ a. become stable earth.
   - ☐ b. often consist of fertile land.
   - ☒ c. may someday begin moving again.

8. The author implies that
   - ☐ a. landslides are more common in Europe than in America.
   - ☐ b. mudslides can be controlled with dams.
   - ☒ c. landslides can be predicted.

9. According to the author, it would not be unusual for a mudflow to
   - ☒ a. bury an automobile.
   - ☐ b. cause an earthquake.
   - ☐ c. occur during a time of drought.

10. We can conclude that buildings
    - ☐ a. should not be constructed on mountain slopes.
    - ☒ b. can be designed to reduce the danger of landslides.
    - ☐ c. should be constructed of stone in mountainous areas.

People get together in groups for many different reasons. Their purpose could be anything from playing a game of basketball to learning to speak Chinese. A therapy group is made up of people who aren't happy with their lives or aren't doing as well as they could because of problems involving their thoughts and feelings. Their purpose is to learn to get along better with themselves and others and to develop healthier, better ways of dealing with life's difficulties and challenges. "Group therapy" is a term for the process they go through as they, and their leader, work together to reach this goal.

Medical historians trace the beginning of group therapy back to 1905, when a Boston physician started to bring tuberculosis patients together in a weekly class that included some discussion of personal problems relating to their disease. During the 1920s and 1930s, several psychiatrists experimented with group methods for treating mental and emotional difficulties. After World War II, however, the idea and practice of group therapy really began to spread.

When the war ended, many veterans needed psychiatric help. The general public, too, became increasingly aware that psychotherapy could help troubled people. There were not enough specialists to meet the demand for treatment. And the cost on an individual basis, was far beyond the average person's ability to pay. By working with groups, therapists could make help available to more people at less cost.

Although some individuals and some problems are not well suited to group treatment, many specialists feel that in other cases the group method has certain definite advantages over a one-to-one, patient-therapist approach.

Membership in the American Group Psychotherapy Association, an organization with entrance requirements based on education and training, has grown from less than 20 in 1942 to well over 3,000 members. This figure represents only a fraction of the number involved in forming or leading therapy groups throughout the country.

Today, group therapy offers help to many people from many different walks of life. Some of the problems dealt with may be very complicated or troublesome; alcoholism, drug addiction, family or marital problems. Other problems may have resulted from a person having low self-esteem or difficulty dealing with other people. It is much more socially acceptable today to be involved in group or individual therapy. Young or old, married or single—almost anyone can benefit from group therapy.

Recalling Facts

1. Medical historians trace the origins of group therapy to
   - ☑ a. 1905.
   - ☐ b. 1925.
   - ☐ c. 1945.

2. The first group therapy patients were suffering from
   - ☐ a. schizophrenia.
   - ☑ b. tuberculosis.
   - ☐ c. polio.

3. Meeting in groups rather than one-to-one
   - ☑ a. reduces tensions.
   - ☐ b. lowers costs.
   - ☐ c. establishes friendships.

4. The American Group Psychotherapy Association has grown to over
   - ☐ a. 500 members.
   - ☑ b. 3,000 members.
   - ☐ c. 6,000 members.

5. The first group therapy sessions were held weekly in
   - ☑ a. Boston.
   - ☐ b. Philadelphia.
   - ☐ c. Chicago.

Understanding the Passage

6. A therapy group is comprised of people who are
   - ☐ a. paranoic.
   - ☐ b. insecure.
   - ☑ c. unhappy.

7. The author implies that
   - ☐ a. war can cause psychiatric problems.
   - ☐ b. therapy groups are usually restricted to six people.
   - ☑ c. most group members are alcoholics and drug addicts.

8. From the article, we can assume that
   - ☐ a. children are excluded from most discussion groups.
   - ☑ b. husbands and wives often attend therapy sessions together.
   - ☐ c. elderly patients are often reluctant to speak in sessions.

9. The American Group Psychotherapy Association
   - ☐ a. is a branch of the American Medical Association.
   - ☐ b. has offices in several foreign countries.
   - ☑ c. does not represent the majority of group therapists.

10. We can conclude that
    - ☑ a. revealing personal problems to others is effective therapy.
    - ☐ b. therapy counseling is free of charge to veterans.
    - ☐ c. college credit is given for participation in therapy.

42   Pollution Problems

The water that flows into a lake or from a river into the ocean reflects everything that happens on the land within the drainage basin, or watershed, of that lake or river. Correction of a pollution problem in a river must, therefore, consist of an integrated approach that will include corrective measures for all sources within the river basin.

Most river basins contain large areas of agricultural lands. The degree of pollution from livestock and agricultural chemicals will vary in different parts of the country according to the type of agriculture being practiced. Contamination of waters by industry will also depend upon the types of industry located within the basin as well as upon the degree of industrial development.

Urban pollution, primarily from sewage disposal, will vary with population distribution and concentration and the degree of effective sewage treatment.

Water problems in the future will become more intense and more complex. Our growing population will tremendously increase urban wastes, primarily sewage. On the other hand, increasing demands for water will decrease substantially the amount of water available for diluting wastes. Rapidly expanding industries that involve more and more complex chemical processes will produce larger volumes of effluents, and many of these will contain chemicals that are either toxic or noxious. To feed our rapidly expanding population, agriculture will have to be intensified. This will involve ever-increasing quantities of agricultural chemicals. From this, it is apparent that drastic steps must be taken immediately to develop corrective measures for the pollution problem.

There are two ways by which this pollution problem can be mitigated. The first relates to the treatment of wastes to decrease their pollution hazard. This involves the processing of solid wastes prior to disposal and the treatment of liquid wastes, or effluents, to permit the reuse of the water or minimize pollution upon final disposal.

A second approach is to develop an economic use for all or a part of the wastes. Farm manure is spread in fields as a nutrient and organic supplement. Effluents from sewage disposal plants are used in some areas both for irrigation and for the nutrients contained. Effluents from other processing plants may also be used as a supplemental source of water. Many industries, such as meat and poultry processing plants, are currently converting former waste products into marketable byproducts. Other industries are exploring potential economic uses for their waste products.

Recalling Facts

1. Most river basins contain
   large areas of land that are
   - ☒ a. agricultural.
   - ☐ b. commercial.
   - ☐ c. residential.

2. Water problems in the future
   will be
   - ☐ a. less severe.
   - ☐ b. eliminated.
   - ☒ c. more complex.

3. Effluents are being used in
   some areas as
   - ☐ a. inexpensive fuel.
   - ☐ b. animal feed.
   - ☒ c. supplemental irrigation.

4. A primary source of urban
   pollution is
   - ☐ a. garbage.
   - ☐ b. detergents.
   - ☒ c. sewage.

5. How many solutions to the
   water pollution problem
   are offered?
   - ☒ a. two
   - ☐ b. three
   - ☐ c. four

Understanding the Passage

6. The purpose of this selection is to
   - ☐ a. acquaint the reader with
     water pollution problems.
   - ☒ b. alert the reader to the
     dwindling water supply.
   - ☐ c. explain industrial uses
     of water.

7. The author implies that
   correcting a pollution problem
   in a river
   - ☐ a. can be a dangerous job.
   - ☒ b. necessitates a survey of
     land areas.
   - ☐ c. requires a careful study of
     underwater plant growth.

8. This selection could be labeled
   - ☐ a. argumentation.
   - ☒ b. exposition.
   - ☐ c. narration.

9. The author gives substance to the
   selection through the use of
   - ☐ a. interviews with authorities in
     the field of water controls.
   - ☐ b. definitions that clarify
     important terms.
   - ☒ c. opinions and personal
     observations.

10. The reader can conclude that
    - ☒ a. some industries are now making
      economic use of wastes.
    - ☐ b. countries of the world will work
      together on pollution problems.
    - ☐ c. science is making great progress
      on increasing water supplies.

43 Keeping Cool

In the lexicon of violent activities, a cold-blooded deed is one conceived and carried out as dispassionately as a lizard catches a fly. Cold-bloodedness is repugnant to mammals and birds, for they, like humans, are warm-blooded creatures that maintain an essentially constant body temperature regardless of the thermal environment.

To keep on the cool side of their upper thermal limits, human bodies dissipate heat by varying the rate and depth of blood circulation, by losing water through the skin and sweat glands, and, as the last extremity is reached, by panting. Under normal conditions, these reflex activities are kept in balance and controlled by the brain's hypothalamus, a comparatively simple sensor of rising and falling environmental temperatures. It is also a sophisticated manager of temperatures inside.

Like the hot light in a car, the hypothalamus responds to the temperature of the coolant, which in this case is blood. A surge of blood heated above 98.6 degrees sends the hypothalamus into action. As orders of the hypothalamus go out, the heart begins to pump more blood, blood vessels dilate to accommodate the increased flow, and the bundles of tiny capillaries threading through the upper layers of the skin are put into operation. The body's blood is circulated closer to the skin's surface, and excess heat drains off into the cooler atmosphere. At the same time, water diffuses through the skin as insensible perspiration, so called because it evaporates before it becomes visible, and the skin seems dry to the touch.

Heat loss from increased circulation and insensible perspiration is a comparatively minor correction. If the hypothalamus continues to sense overheating, it calls upon the millions of sweat glands that perforate the outer layer of the skin. These tiny glands can shed great quantities of water and heat through perspiration. The skin handles about 90 percent of the body's heat-dissipating function.

As environmental temperature approaches normal body temperature, physical discomfort is replaced by physical danger. The body loses its ability to get rid of heat through the circulatory system, because there is no heat-drawing drop in temperature between the skin and the surrounding air. At this point, the skin's elimination of heat by sweating becomes virtually the only means of maintaining constant temperature. Sweating, by itself, does nothing to cool the body, unless the water is removed by evaporation. High relative humidity retards evaporation.

---

*Reading Time*_____ *Comprehension Score*_____ *Words per Minute*_____ 99

Recalling Facts

1. Heat is dissipated most effectively by
   - ☐ a. panting.
   - ☑ b. perspiration.
   - ☐ c. dilation of the arteries.

2. The temperature of the body is controlled by the
   - ☑ a. hypothalamus.
   - ☐ b. cortex.
   - ☐ c. cerebrum.

3. Insensible perspiration
   - ☐ a. cannot be felt.
   - ☑ b. is caused by nervousness.
   - ☐ c. indicates illness.

4. What percentage of body heat is dissipated by the skin?
   - ☐ a. 30 percent
   - ☐ b. 60 percent
   - ☑ c. 90 percent

5. Which one of the following animals is warm-blooded?
   - ☐ a. a snake
   - ☐ b. a fish
   - ☑ c. a bird

Understanding the Passage

6. According to the author, warm-blooded animals
   - ☑ a. maintain a constant body temperature.
   - ☐ b. have body temperatures above 98 degrees.
   - ☐ c. prefer warm climates.

7. Sweating will lower the body's temperature if
   - ☐ a. a person is at rest.
   - ☐ b. the heart pumps faster.
   - ☑ c. relative humidity is low.

8. This article is concerned primarily with
   - ☐ a. physical fitness through exercise.
   - ☐ b. the regulatory functions of the brain.
   - ☑ c. ways the body regulates to temperatures.

9. The circulatory system loses its ability to cool the body when
   - ☑ a. environmental temperatures approach 100 degrees.
   - ☐ b. breathing is restricted.
   - ☐ c. clothing is too tight.

10. We can conclude that
    - ☑ a. the body is a sensitive mechanism.
    - ☐ b. most warm-blooded animals cannot survive high temperatures.
    - ☑ c. exercise can increase the heart's ability to pump blood.

The idea of mounting a theatrical production is almost universally appealing. Just think of those old movies where some neighborhood kid would rally others for blocks around with the cry "Let's put on a show!" In the popular imagination, acting is a natural talent, and "putting on a show" is as simple as gathering some actors together, developing a story line, and waiting for the ovation.

In reality, producing a play is a complicated undertaking, from both the artistic and the business perspective. Actors are not the only artists involved in preparing the show. In addition to the director, there will be set, lighting, and costume designers, and possibly an assistant director, choreographer, music director, sound designer, or others. In a professional theater, the usual rehearsal period is five weeks, six days a week, during which time not only do the actors learn the lines and develop their characters, but also the designers meet with the director to discuss the image the show is to present. And backstage, the production staff is working equally hard. There are people building the sets and costumes, searching for props, hanging lights, and a technical director organizing and monitoring the whole operation.

Even this is not the full picture. Whether or not the theater is large enough to hire a managing director or to have a business office, someone must attend to the decidedly unglamorous business aspects of the production. Handling the box office and marketing areas alone can be a full time responsibility. Someone has to order the tickets, take and confirm reservations, approach groups for possible group discount packages, contact subscribers, and staff the box office for each performance, including dealing with exchanges and charges.

Public relations is another major area of responsibility. Since only the wealthiest theaters can afford paid advertising, public relations people must be creative and persevering in order to maintain a high public profile for the theater. This includes developing public service announcements, which will be run for free on radio and television, cultivating a positive relationship with local reporters and critics, writing press releases, and working with graphic artists and printers so posters, programs, and mailings are completed in a timely fashion.

Whole books could—and have—been written about other aspects of theater management, such as house management, concessions, finances, and building maintenance. So, the next time you applaud a play, add a cheer for all the people behind the scenes.

Recalling Facts

1. In addition to the actors and director, the artists will include
   - ☐ a. set and light designers.
   - ☑ b. an assistant director.
   - ☐ c. a managing director.

2. The usual rehearsal period is
   - ☐ a. one month.
   - ☐ b. five weeks.
   - ☑ c. six weeks.

3. The production staff
   - ☐ a. runs the box office.
   - ☐ b. writes press releases.
   - ☑ c. builds sets and makes costumes.

4. The supervisor of the production staff is called the
   - ☐ a. director.
   - ☐ b. managing director.
   - ☑ c. technical director.

5. The person who approaches groups about discounts is the
   - ☐ a. box office manager.
   - ☑ b. public relations coordinator.
   - ☐ c. managing director.

Understanding the Passage

6. Designers create the sets, lights, and costumes
   - ☑ a. according to the suggestions in the script.
   - ☐ b. from their own artistic vision.
   - ☐ c. after talking to the director about the concept of the show.

7. The phrase "develop their characters" suggests that actors
   - ☐ a. bring a lot of their personal ideas to the role.
   - ☑ b. must learn specific gestures as well as their lines.
   - ☐ c. need special character makeup.

8. A technical director needs knowledge of
   - ☐ a. acting and directing.
   - ☐ b. arts management.
   - ☑ c. set building and time management.

9. The article imples that in a small theater with no paid staff,
   - ☑ a. several active volunteers will be needed.
   - ☐ b. the actors will have to take turns running the box office.
   - ☐ c. it will be impossible to develop public service announcements.

10. Public service announcements are better than advertising because
    - ☐ a. they reach more people.
    - ☑ b. they are free.
    - ☐ c. radio is always better than newspapers.

45　Tribal Law and Order

Indian tribes are recognized in federal law as distinct political groups with basic domestic and municipal functions. These include the power to operate under a form of government of the tribe's choosing. The tribes can define conditions of tribal membership, regulate domestic relations of members, and prescribe rules of inheritance. They are also able to levy taxes, to regulate property within the jurisdiction of the tribe, to administer justice, and to provide for the punishment of offenses committed on the reservation.

The powers of self-government are often exercised according to tribal constitutions and law and order codes. Normally, self-government includes the right of a tribe to define the authority and duties of its officials. It includes the manner of their appointment or election and the manner of their removal.

Those rights are subject to congressional change, as are all functions of tribal rule. For example, federal law has removed from some Oklahoma tribes the power to choose their own officials.

Along with the power to make laws and regulations for the administration of justice, tribes also have the power to maintain law enforcement departments and courts. Some smaller tribes have very informal courts based on old customs, or have no courts at all. Larger tribes, such as the Navaho, have complex law and order systems with well-equipped police departments, modern tribal codes, and a system of trial and appellate courts overseen by a tribal supreme court.

Generally, Indian courts have power over matters involving tribal affairs. The courts have power over civil suits brought by Indians or non-Indians against tribal members on the reservation and over the prosecution of violations of the tribal criminal code.

Federal and state courts have no power over matters involving violations of tribal ordinances. With regard to cases within their jurisdiction, tribal courts are the courts of the last resort. Their decisions cannot be appealed to state or federal courts.

Congress has placed several important limits on tribal power. Under the 1968 Civil Rights Act, tribes may not exercise jurisdiction over criminal offenses punishable by more than a $500 fine or six months in jail. Federal courts have jurisdiction to try and to punish such major offenses as murder, manslaughter, and rape.

In certain instances, Congress has extended state laws to Indian reservations. States that have assumed responsibility for the administration of justice on Indian land are referred to as "Public Law 280 States."

Recalling Facts

1. Federal law allows Indian tribes to
   - ■ a. levy taxes.
   - ☐ b. print money.
   - ☐ c. sacrifice animals.

2. The right to choose their own officials has been taken from some
   - ☐ a. Florida tribes.
   - ☐ b. Oklahoma tribes.
   - ■ c. Idaho tribes.

3. The Navaho tribe is
   - ■ a. large.
   - ☐ b. unique.
   - ☐ c. reactionary.

4. The Civil Rights Act was passed in
   - ☐ a. 1957.
   - ■ b. 1968.
   - ☐ c. 1971.

5. Tribal fines cannot exceed
   - ■ a. $500.
   - ☐ b. $1,000.
   - ☐ c. $5,000.

Understanding the Passage

6. According to the author, decisions made in Indian courts
   - ☐ a. can be appealed in state courts.
   - ☐ b. can be overruled in the Supreme Court.
   - ■ c. cannot be appealed in other courts.

7. The law creating "Public Law 280 States" is concerned with
   - ☐ a. limiting tribal power.
   - ■ b. federal jurisdiction over Indian affairs.
   - ☐ c. extending state laws to Indian reservations.

8. Indian courts have the power to
   - ☐ a. convict a murderer.
   - ■ b. refuse tribal membership to an Indian.
   - ☐ c. deal with incidents occurring outside the reservation.

9. The Navaho system of law and order
   - ■ a. is patterned after the federal system.
   - ☐ b. appears unorthodox to most people.
   - ☐ c. is more advanced than most state governments.

10. We can conclude that
   - ■ a. federal and state governments cooperate with Indian governments.
   - ☐ b. Indians do not pay federal income taxes.
   - ☐ c. Indian children do not receive a proper education.

46   The Insect Hordes

Insects are man's greatest competitor for food and fiber. They are the transmitters of such ancient pestilences as malaria, sleeping sickness, yellow fever, and bubonic plague. These threats to our public health and agricultural abundance are held in check only through the determination of the entomologist and the versatility of the organic chemist.

A major breakthrough in the development of organic pesticides was the discovery and application of DDT in 1939. So effective was DDT in early studies that many predicted the eventual eradication of several insect species. However, they did not reckon with the ability of insects to develop resistance.

Undaunted, the organic chemists proceeded to synthesize the chemical relatives of DDT and other chemicals, some of which were even more toxic to insects than DDT. Toxicants were discovered which provided the farmer and the public health official with undreamed of weapons against the insect hordes. Inexorably, however, the insects retaliated with their extensive capacity to evolve strains resistant to most or all insecticides. Recently, the development of more precise and sensitive methods of analysis for pesticide residues has revealed a disturbing persistence of some of these chemicals in our environment.

Most pesticides are not only toxic to insects, but also to other animals and man. Concern about our environmental health and wildlife and the problem of increasing insecticide resistance requires a new approach to insect control. The agricultural and health demands of our society will not permit a return to methods of control used before 1959. Thus, more fundamental approaches to insect control must be found. The biological, biochemical, and behavioral differences which set insects apart from other animals must be sought after and understood. A study of insect life, feeding, growth, development, and reproduction must be made in order to understand the fundamental differences between insects and other animals. Such a study will permit the development of selective tools for insect control uncomplicated by eventual insect resistance and the potential hazard to human populations.

One such approach to insect control is the application of our rapidly expanding knowledge of how insects rely upon hormones to regulate their growth, feeding, mating, reproduction, and diapause—a state akin to hibernation. Experimental tampering with the hormone-producing machinery can cause an immature insect to stop developing, or to grow too fast. Most of these effects result in the insect's premature death.

Recalling Facts

1. Insects can infect man with
   - ☐ a. scarlet fever.
   - ☐ b. pneumonia.
   - ☒ c. malaria.

2. DDT was discovered in the late
   - ☒ a. 1920s.
   - ☐ b. 1930s.
   - ☐ c. 1940s.

3. DDT is described as
   - ☐ a. an organic pesticide.
   - ☐ b. an inert pesticide.
   - ☒ c. a synthetic pesticide.

4. According to the author, DDT is a
   - ☒ a. hormone regulator.
   - ☐ b. toxic substance.
   - ☐ c. biochemical stabilizer.

5. So effective was DDT in early studies that some scientists predicted
   - ☒ a. eventual eradication of several insect species.
   - ☐ b. increased importance of organic gardening.
   - ☐ c. future dissatisfaction with natural fertilizers.

Understanding the Passage

6. The author feels that the best way to control insects is with
   - ☐ a. biochemical warfare.
   - ☒ b. hormone stimulators.
   - ☐ c. synthetic compounds.

7. One drawback to the use of DDT is that it
   - ☐ a. does not dissolve readily.
   - ☐ b. loses its lethal qualities soon after it is applied.
   - ☒ c. leaves a harmful residue.

8. According to the article, an entomologist studies
   - ☐ a. diseases.
   - ☒ b. insects.
   - ☐ c. farming techniques.

9. The reader can assume that
   - ☐ a. DDT is the strongest insecticide made.
   - ☒ b. several insecticides are similar to DDT in their chemical structures.
   - ☐ c. the formula for DDT was discovered by accident.

10. Scientists who first studied DDT did not anticipate that
    - ☐ a. it would kill many varieties of plants.
    - ☐ b. it would pollute the atmosphere.
    - ☒ c. many insects would become immune to it.

Hospitality as a Business

More and more people travel, for a variety of reasons. Many are tourists, but many venture forth on personal or professional business. Whatever the reason for traveling, a common complaint of travelers is the impersonal accommodations they find.

After spending five consecutive nights in five cookie-cutter hotels, the business traveler may find it difficult to remember what happened from day to day, or even what towns were visited. And the tourist may get the mistaken impression that all cities are pretty much the same, at least as far as decor, food, and service are concerned.

To combat this sense of impersonal sameness, travelers are taking ●
advantage of in-home hospitality, or Bed & Breakfast arrangements. B&Bs are private homes which offer lodging and breakfast in a very personalized, friendly setting. For decades, B&Bs have been the classic way to visit Europe, especially the British Isles. And in fact, they are not really a new idea in America. The tradition dates back to colonial times when inns were few and far between, and the weary traveler had to depend on the kindness of strangers for a meal and a bed. But the resurgence of B&Bs as ●
desirable accommodations is a fairly recent phenomenon.

If the idea of operating a B&B piques your interest, there are several factors to consider before plunging into this business. The first consideration is your property, not only the building itself, but the location. If you live near a famous historical site, or in a popular destination, such as New York City or Washington, D.C., your home can be fairly simple, yet still do well as a B&B. On the other hand, if your home is architecturally unique, or has amenities for the traveler such as a private entrance, private bath, or swimming pool, people may be willing to go a bit farther afield to reach you. ●

Another important factor is the life-style of you and your family. You must take into account whether all members of the family truly enjoy visitors, want to repeatedly discuss local sights and activities, and have the time and energy to handle the additional cooking, cleaning, laundry, and bookkeeping involved.

The final consideration is a financial one. Potential Bed & Breakfast hosts must be realistic about opportunities for income. While B&Bs usually have low initial costs, experts estimate it would take at least five rooms rented regularly for the host to earn a living from a B&B.

Recalling Facts

1. A common complaint of travelers is
   - ☐ a. a lack of B&Bs in America.
   - ☐ b. expensive accommodations.
   - ☒ c. impersonal accommodations.

2. Bed & Breakfast lodgings are usually located in
   - ☐ a. private homes.
   - ☐ b. major tourist areas.
   - ☒ c. country inns.

3. In the U.S., the idea of B&Bs can be said to date from
   - ☐ a. the 1920s.
   - ☐ b. the 18th century.
   - ☒ c. colonial times.

4. The most important aspects of your home as a B&B include
   - ☒ a. a private bath and private entrance.
   - ☐ b. location and architectural interest.
   - ☐ c. living in New York or Washington, D.C.

5. Financially, B&Bs provide
   - ☐ a. a lucrative income.
   - ☐ b. a steady living.
   - ☒ c. limited income, but limited costs also.

Understanding the Passage

6. In this article, a "cookie-cutter hotel" describes
   - ☐ a. a small hotel with cute trim.
   - ☒ b. a hotel which is just like many others.
   - ☐ c. an inn specializing in bakery.

7. Colonial B&Bs were most likely
   - ☐ a. similar to contemporary hospitality businesses.
   - ☒ b. very small and cramped.
   - ☐ c. not really a business, but a friendly gesture.

8. The article implies that the idea of starting a B&B
   - ☒ a. should be thoroughly discussed by all members of the family.
   - ☐ b. is not really worth all the trouble.
   - ☐ c. is a good idea only if local hotels aren't very good.

9. A traveler might want to stay at a B&B because
   - ☐ a. it's fun to look at other people's houses.
   - ☒ b. it gives them a chance to talk with people about the area.
   - ☐ c. it's cheaper than a hotel.

10. If you don't have at least five rooms available,
    - ☒ a. a B&B can still be a fun way to earn extra income.
    - ☐ b. there's no point to even trying a B&B.
    - ☐ c. you need to live in a very desirable location to open a B&B.

When the early pioneers pushed westward across the prairies, deserts, and rugged mountains, they found one common characteristic—drought. Because of scant or irregular rainfall throughout most of the West, potentially fertile land needed additional water to fulfill its promise of abundant crops. Simple diversion was undertaken to supply water to the thirsty acres, but it did not solve the problem of erratic riverflow. The water reached flood proportions when the snows melted, but by summer there was hardly more than a trickle.

Dams were needed to regulate the flow and to store the water during times of high runoff so that it could be used in periods of drought. To help meet this need, the National Reclamation Act was passed in 1902, opening the way for the Bureau of Reclamation to construct dams, reservoirs, and canal systems that now make irrigation available to more than ten million acres in the seventeen contiguous western states.

The multipurpose reclamation program contributes significantly to the nation's economic strength because it furnishes water for municipal and industrial growth. Crops grown on its projects comprise an important part of our healthful diet. A stabilized farm economy provides a foundation for industrial development of the West and other sections of the country as well. Pollution-free hydropower supplies energy, and the aggregate prosperity thus born has established substantial tax bases to enrich the federal, state, and local governmental treasuries.

The benefits of recreation, too, can be calculated in a financial ledger, reporting the monetary returns of a soaring tourist business. However, the most valuable aspects of reclamation's recreation dividends are the intangibles of mental and physical well-being. How can we put a price tag on a fisherman's joy at hooking a prize fish, or a nature lover's delight as he explores the outdoors, whether it be an awesome canyon, a lofty mountain peak, or a sparkling lake?

Enthusiasm of Americans for outdoor recreation reflects the changing living patterns of today's society. Surrounded by asphalt, brick, and all the other trappings of civilization, modern man sees his opportunities to enjoy nature diminishing at an alarming rate. More than ever before, he needs that sustenance for his spirit, as well as for his body, that he derives from a relationship with nature. Yet, urban sprawl and industrial development, with their attendant misuse of the land and pollution of the water, are defacing the countryside that once seemed limitless.

Recalling Facts

1. One problem the pioneers found as they moved West was
   ☐ a. poverty.
   ☑ b. drought.
   ☐ c. danger.

2. The National Reclamation Act was passed in
   ☑ a. 1902.
   ☐ b. 1935.
   ☐ c. 1961.

3. How much land has been made fertile by the Reclamation Act?
   ☑ a. 5 million acres
   ☐ b. 10 million acres
   ☐ c. 20 million acres

4. The Bureau of Reclamation
   ☐ a. builds dams.
   ☑ b. drains swamps.
   ☐ c. constructs playgrounds.

5. To supply water to their farmlands, the pioneers used the process of
   ☐ a. reclamation.
   ☑ b. diversion.
   ☐ c. storage.

Understanding the Passage

6. This article is concerned primarily with
   ☐ a. early exploration of the West.
   ☑ b. the work of the Bureau of Reclamation.
   ☐ c. legislation that protects the national forests.

7. According to the article,
   ☐ a. unspoiled land is rapidly disappearing.
   ☐ b. agriculture is polluting the nation's water.
   ☑ c. industry determines patterns of living.

8. The author implies that
   ☐ a. a stable farm economy is the basis for industrial growth.
   ☐ b. electricity is less expensive in the West.
   ☑ c. pioneers knew that industry would deface the land.

9. The author appears to be mildly critical of
   ☑ a. the trappings of civilization.
   ☐ b. dam construction in the West.
   ☐ c. hydroelectric pollution.

10. We can conclude that
    ☑ a. the pioneers established the dominant spirit in the U.S. today.
    ☑ b. the National Reclamation Act helps the U.S. economy.
    ☐ c. People in the U.S. are overly concerned with recreation.

The free enterprise system has produced a technology capable of providing the American consumer with the largest and most varied marketplace in the world. Technological advances, however, have come hand-in-hand with impersonal mass marketing of goods and services. Along with progress, too, have come some instances of manipulative advertising practices and a proliferation of products whose reliability, safety, and quality are difficult to evaluate.

Today's consumers buy, enjoy, use, and discard more types of goods than could possibly have been imagined even a few years ago. Yet too often consumers are as unaware of the materials that have gone into the manufacturer's finished product as they are of their own motivation in selecting one product over another.

Easy credit and the forceful techniques of modern marketing persuade many consumers to buy what they cannot afford. The consequent overburdening of family budgets is a problem for consumers at all economic levels. It is not unusual for families to allocate 20 percent or more of their income to debt repayments without understanding the effect this allocation has upon other choices. Some families have such tight budgets that an illness, a period of unemployment, or some other crisis finds them without adequate reserves. In addition to the growing complexity of the market, consumers are sometimes faced with unfair and deceptive practices. Although there are laws designed to protect the consumer, there is not a sufficient number of law enforcers to cover all the abuses of the marketplace.

There is growing concern and awareness today of the disadvantage of the poor and undereducated American in the marketplace of the affluent. Families in low-income inner city and rural areas often do not have access to the same varieties of goods and prices as their middle-income counterparts do. Furthermore, they are more likely to be targets for fraudulent sales schemes and high cost credit than their affluent neighbors.

An adult in today's society should be educated in the sensible use of credit. He should understand what is involved in purchasing a house, and the many pitfalls to be avoided when entering into financial agreements. He should know enough about advertising and selling techniques to be able to discern the honest from the fraudulent and deceptive. He should be knowledgeable about consumer protection laws so that he can demand his rights. When he needs help, he should know about the private and public sources to which he can turn for assistance.

Recalling Facts

1. According to the author, many families overspend by
   ☑ a. 20 percent.
   ☐ b. 30 percent.
   ☐ c. 40 percent.

2. The author feels that the American marketplace is
   ☑ a. overrated.
   ☐ b. inefficient.
   ☐ c. complex.

3. The person who suffers most in the American marketplace is the
   ☑ a. affluent buyer.
   ☐ b. unwise shopper.
   ☐ c. foreign investor.

4. The weakness inherent in the laws designed to protect the consumer is the
   ☐ a. large number of loopholes.
   ☐ b. insufficient number of law enforcers.
   ☑ c. lack of prohibitive penalties.

5. As technology has advanced, mass marketing has become
   ☑ a. impersonal.
   ☐ b. formal.
   ☐ c. reliable.

Understanding the Passage

6. This article is concerned mostly with
   ☐ a. the free enterprise system in America.
   ☑ b. the difficulty of living on a fixed income.
   ☐ c. innovative techniques in food processing.

7. The author implies that
   ☐ a. products are more expensive in the United States.
   ☐ b. credit cards are often used illegally.
   ☑ c. products very often do not perform as advertised.

8. Consumers often do not know
   ☐ a. the brand names of products they buy regularly.
   ☐ b. the current interest rates on savings accounts.
   ☑ c. why they purchase certain products.

9. The author points out that some families
   ☑ a. are unprepared for financial emergencies.
   ☐ b. forget to claim interest charges on their tax forms.
   ☐ c. spend more money on food than they would like to.

10. The author warns the reader to be cautious when buying items
    ☐ a. on sale.
    ☑ b. on credit.
    ☐ c. at a discount.

A Providential Vacation

When it comes time to select a vacation site, do various members of your family have conflicting priorities? You may be attracted to the excitement of a metropolitan area, your spouse may prefer spending quiet time in the great outdoors, and the children may be looking for something new to do that will keep them occupied.

Providence, Rhode Island is a destination you should consider which will match every one of these interests. Providence may not be readily identified as a vacation spot by most people, but being somewhat undiscovered only adds to its desirability, because travelers don't have to battle crowds and wait in long lines.

For those who enjoy the bustle of a city, Providence has a lot to offer. Although small, with only 200,000 inhabitants, it supports a major regional theater and half a dozen semi-professional stage companies. A huge, historic theater and an arena regularly host dance ensembles, orchestras, rock and popular musicians, and Broadway shows.

Providence is home to Brown University, a large Ivy League campus, the internationally renowned Rhode Island School of Design, and other small colleges. These not only offer lovely walks among historic buildings, but also provide cultural enrichment for the city.

There are popular shopping areas, featuring boutiques, gourmet shops and cafés, and other specialty stores. Right in the heart of downtown stands the Arcade, with its wrought iron banisters and vaulted skylights, built in 1828 as America's first enclosed shopping mall.

The restaurants of Providence are exquisite, featuring not only native seafood, but international culinary delights including Portuguese, Thai, Cambodian, Indian, and Armenian. Providence is also home to several world class, award-winning chefs who offer their own unique creations.

For the person who prefers a peaceful afternoon in the countryside, Providence is conveniently located within minutes of several state parks, ocean beaches, and wildlife refuges, and it is only a few hours from the woods and mountains of the other New England states. Without even leaving the city limits, you can spend all day in Roger Williams Park, over 450 acres encompassing flower gardens, Japanese gardens, lakes, a zoo, and a natural history museum.

And if the park isn't enough to keep the children occupied for the whole trip, there are other places especially for them. In neighboring towns are a children's museum with touchable, interactive exhibits, and two working carousels, one more than a hundred years old.

Recalling Facts

1. The population of Providence is
   - [ ] a. 150,000.
   - [x] b. 200,000.
   - [ ] c. 250,000.

2. The Arcade is a
   - [ ] a. major regional theater.
   - [ ] b. popular restaurant.
   - [x] c. shopping mall.

3. The large educational institution in Providence is
   - [ ] a. Rhode Island School of Design.
   - [ ] b. Providence College.
   - [x] c. Brown University.

4. The nearest mountains are located in
   - [ ] a. other New England states.
   - [ ] b. Roger Williams Park.
   - [x] c. state parks.

5. Roger Williams Park has
   - [ ] a. ocean beaches.
   - [ ] b. a hundred-year-old carousel.
   - [x] c. a zoo.

Understanding the Passage

6. Providence's size makes it a good vacation spot because
   - [ ] a. there are more theaters per capita than in larger cities.
   - [ ] b. you can save cab fare by walking.
   - [x] c. there are many good places without the crowds of larger cities.

7. The Arcade is worth a visit because
   - [x] a. it has as many stores as the suburban shopping malls.
   - [ ] b. it has unique architecture and historic value.
   - [ ] c. you can find good bargains there.

8. For a city of its size, Providence has an unusual number of
   - [x] a. restaurants.
   - [ ] b. dance ensembles.
   - [ ] c. theaters.

9. If the children's museum had an exhibit of puppets,
   - [x] a. the children could play with them and make their own.
   - [ ] b. there would be a puppet show.
   - [ ] c. there would be many kinds of puppets.

10. The famous chefs of Providence
    - [x] a. specialize in New England cuisine.
    - [ ] b. develop their own recipes.
    - [ ] c. run expensive restaurants.

114

Answer Key

Progress Graph

Pacing Graph

Answer Key

	1.	2.	3.	4.	5.	6.	7.	8.	9.	10.
1	b	c	a	c	a	b	c	c	c	a
2	c	a	b	a	b	a	c	b	c	a
3	a	c	b	a	c	c	c	a	c	c
4	c	c	a	b	b	c	a	b	b	a
5	a	c	c	a	b	b	b	a	a	c
6	c	c	b	c	c	b	a	c	a	b
7	a	a	c	a	c	c	b	b	c	c
8	c	a	b	c	b	a	b	c	c	a
9	b	a	b	c	c	a	b	c	a	c
10	b	a	b	c	a	c	a	b	a	c
11	b	c	a	c	a	b	c	b	c	a
12	b	a	c	c	b	c	b	b	c	a
13	b	b	b	a	b	a	c	c	c	b
14	b	c	b	b	c	c	a	b	a	a
15	c	a	b	c	b	b	b	a	b	a
16	b	a	c	c	a	c	b	b	a	b
17	a	c	a	c	c	b	c	a	c	a
18	c	c	a	c	b	b	a	a	b	c
19	c	b	a	c	b	a	b	c	c	a
20	a	c	a	a	a	a	a	c	b	a
21	a	b	b	c	b	a	c	c	a	c
22	c	b	b	a	a	a	a	b	c	a
23	c	a	c	c	a	b	c	b	a	b
24	a	b	b	a	c	c	c	b	b	c
25	a	c	a	c	a	b	c	b	a	c

26	1. b	2. c	3. c	4. b	5. c	6. c	7. c	8. c	9. b	10. c
27	1. c	2. c	3. b	4. c	5. c	6. c	7. b	8. c	9. b	10. a
28	1. a	2. b	3. a	4. c	5. b	6. a	7. b	8. a	9. c	10. b
29	1. a	2. c	3. c	4. a	5. b	6. b	7. c	8. a	9. c	10. a
30	1. a	2. a	3. c	4. b	5. b	6. c	7. c	8. c	9. b	10. a
31	1. a	2. b	3. c	4. c	5. c	6. a	7. a	8. a	9. b	10. a
32	1. a	2. b	3. a	4. b	5. c	6. c	7. c	8. b	9. a	10. b
33	1. c	2. c	3. c	4. b	5. b	6. a	7. c	8. c	9. a	10. c
34	1. a	2. c	3. b	4. c	5. a	6. b	7. c	8. b	9. c	10. b
35	1. c	2. c	3. c	4. a	5. b	6. a	7. a	8. c	9. b	10. c
36	1. b	2. b	3. a	4. a	5. c	6. c	7. c	8. c	9. a	10. a
37	1. a	2. c	3. c	4. a	5. c	6. a	7. a	8. b	9. b	10. b
38	1. c	2. a	3. c	4. b	5. c	6. b	7. c	8. c	9. a	10. c
39	1. c	2. c	3. a	4. a	5. c	6. b	7. c	8. a	9. c	10. b
40	1. b	2. a	3. b	4. b	5. b	6. c	7. c	8. c	9. a	10. b
41	1. a	2. b	3. b	4. b	5. a	6. c	7. a	8. b	9. c	10. a
42	1. a	2. c	3. c	4. c	5. a	6. a	7. b	8. b	9. c	10. a
43	1. b	2. a	3. a	4. c	5. c	6. a	7. c	8. c	9. a	10. a
44	1. a	2. b	3. c	4. c	5. a	6. c	7. a	8. c	9. a	10. b
45	1. a	2. b	3. a	4. b	5. a	6. c	7. c	8. b	9. a	10. a
46	1. c	2. b	3. a	4. b	5. a	6. b	7. c	8. b	9. b	10. c
47	1. c	2. a	3. c	4. b	5. c	6. b	7. c	8. a	9. b	10. a
48	1. b	2. a	3. b	4. a	5. b	6. b	7. a	8. a	9. a	10. b
49	1. a	2. c	3. b	4. b	5. a	6. a	7. c	8. c	9. a	10. b
50	1. b	2. c	3. c	4. a	5. c	6. c	7. b	8. c	9. a	10. b

Progress Graph (1–25)

Directions: Write your comprehension score in the box under the selection number. Then put an x on the line above each box to show your reading time and words-per-minute reading rate.

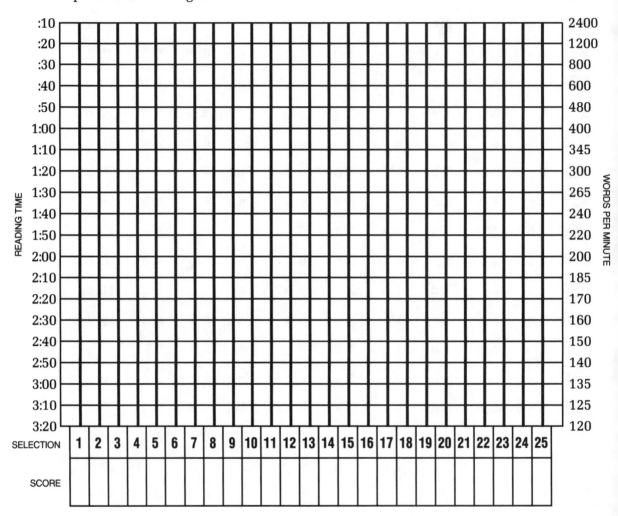

READING TIME		WORDS PER MINUTE
:10		2400
:20		1200
:30		800
:40		600
:50		480
1:00		400
1:10		345
1:20		300
1:30		265
1:40		240
1:50		220
2:00		200
2:10		185
2:20		170
2:30		160
2:40		150
2:50		140
3:00		135
3:10		125
3:20		120

SELECTION: 1 2 3 4 5 6 7 8 9 10 11 12 13 14 15 16 17 18 19 20 21 22 23 24 25

SCORE

118

Progress Graph (26–50)

Directions: Write your comprehension score in the box under the selection number. Then put an x on the line above each box to show your reading time and words-per-minute reading rate.

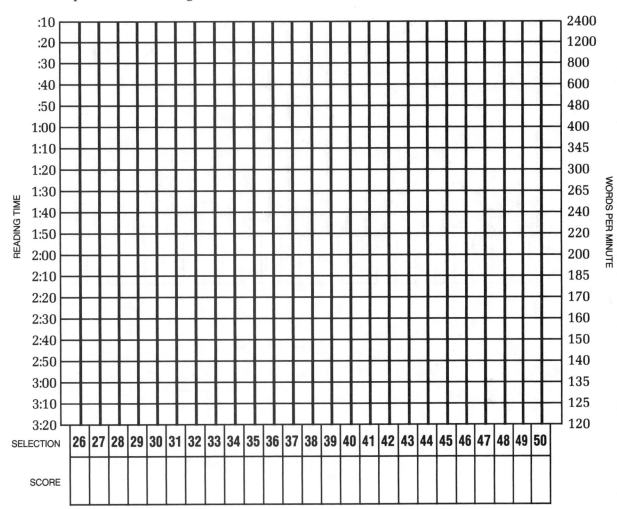

READING TIME		WORDS PER MINUTE
:10		2400
:20		1200
:30		800
:40		600
:50		480
1:00		400
1:10		345
1:20		300
1:30		265
1:40		240
1:50		220
2:00		200
2:10		185
2:20		170
2:30		160
2:40		150
2:50		140
3:00		135
3:10		125
3:20		120

SELECTION	26	27	28	29	30	31	32	33	34	35	36	37	38	39	40	41	42	43	44	45	46	47	48	49	50
SCORE																									

Pacing Graph

Directions: In the boxes labeled "Pace" along the bottom of the graph, write your words-per-minute rate. On the vertical line above each box, put an x to indicate your comprehension score.

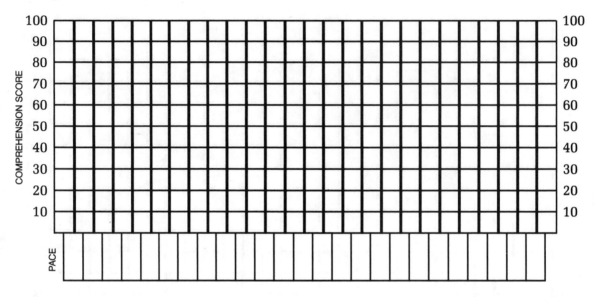